Get Ready to Grow

GET READY TO GROW

A Strategy for
Local Church Growth

by

Paul R. Orjala

Beacon Hill Press of Kansas City
Kansas City, Missouri

Contents

Instructions for Receiving
Christian Service Training Credit

1. This is the text for First Series Unit 160.3a, "Developing a Strategy for Church Growth." Six 50-minute sessions, or the equivalent in time, are required.

2. Your class should be registered with the general office at least three weeks before your first class session. This will allow time for the office to get the class report forms and individual registration slips to you. Also, it will help get texts on time.

3. Each pupil must be present for five of the six sessions and study the text to receive credit.

4. This course may be taken by correspondence.

5. Please send in the class report to the General Christian Service Training Office upon completion of the course.

For further information, consult your local Christian Service Training director or write . . .

CHRISTIAN SERVICE TRAINING
6401 THE PASEO
KANSAS CITY, MO. 64131

Foreword

The "go and make disciples" of the Great Commission has been the chief driving force among Nazarene leaders in preparing this study on church growth.

It is our hope that every church will find a workable philosophy of church growth and recognize clearly the difference between what is true church growth and what is not. A further aim has been to help us discover how the concepts of church management, evangelism, discipleship, and body life contribute to genuine church growth.

Toward this end, the Department of Home Missions has been engaged in extensive research since 1973, seeking the reasons for successful church growth as well as the reasons for the failure of churches that have died. We are now ready to reap the fruit of that research.

Our general and district leaders have given earnest attention to understanding the principles of church growth through a training process given at the highest level of academic scholarship. It is now time for every congregation to intensify this effort through the study of basic principles relating to church growth. It is to this end that we commend this volume, written by Dr. Paul Orjala. Our churches will not grow automatically from the reading of this book. But it is our hope and prayer that the earnest study of the principles portrayed in the book will lead thousands of Nazarene churches to find the key to significant growth in their own demographic setting.

—RAYMOND W. HURN
Executive Director,
Department of Home Missions

7

Preface

Suddenly everyone is talking about "church growth." What is so new about that? It's been going on since Pentecost. But what some people think is "church growth" may turn out to be something else.

It's like the story about a city slicker who visited a farm for the first time. He asked the farmer, "Why doesn't this cow have horns?"

The farmer scratched his head and replied, "Well, some cows never have horns. Other cows have their horns taken off. But the reason this cow doesn't have horns is because this cow is a horse."

The term "church growth" is used in both a technical and nontechnical way. As a technical term, it refers to "church-growth thought" or "the church-growth movement" begun in the 1950s by Dr. Donald A. McGavran and continued and developed today by his students. Dr. McGavran added to biblical and theological understanding of church growth a scientific approach to discover verifiable concepts which account for church growth.

In this book, "church growth" is used both in this technical sense and in the normal sense relating to the way that churches grow.

Dr. McGavran's first concern was to increase the rate and scope of evangelism and church planting on the "mission fields" of the Third World (Africa, Asia, and Latin America). In the 1970s, these transferable concepts began to be applied to the problems of growth in North America.

For the concepts presented in this book, I am heavily indebted to Dr. McGavran, whom I have known personally since 1961, and to his colleagues at the School of World Mission, Pasadena, Calif. I am indebted also to Dr. C. Peter Wagner, vice-president of Fuller Evangelistic Association. It would be impossible to give credit to all to whom it is due. But special thanks is due to the staff of the Department of Home Missions and particularly to John Oster for his invaluable help in editing. The contribution of Dr. Raymond W. Hurn, who supplied the illustrations from growing churches and basic research on Nazarene denominational growth, has almost reached the point where a coauthorship should be acknowledged. This book is really a product of the team effort of the people involved.

How to Use This Book

This book focuses on the local church. It is concerned with what laymen need to know about church growth. There are other more technical books; this book is for everyone who believes God's church should grow.

Whole congregations should study this book and discuss it. Then they should study their own church and community and take action to implement the concepts. It does no more good to learn *about* church-growth concepts without putting them into practice than to study *about* a language and never learn to speak it. *Church growth must not turn out to be our hobby; it must be our passion.*

Make this study a whole-church project, studying the book in prayer meeting, a chapter a week, for six weeks. Begin by appointing a church-growth committee which can do the necessary research.

Be sure to get the whole church involved—studying, discussing, praying, and planning—for each department of the church. Each week, let church leaders discuss the

9

current chapter with their department people to discover its application to their sphere of activity. Let the discussion get into Sunday school classes, youth meetings, the missionary societies, and church board meetings. Let the prayer life of the church be directed toward church growth. And let the church start planning and applying aspects of each chapter immediately following its study.

The Basic Church-Growth Library

There are four books, all available in paperback editions through the Nazarene Publishing House, which have valuable additional information not included in this book. Every church is urged to buy them all in order to have them available for reference and reading for further church-growth study. They are listed in the order of their importance and usefulness for the local church. The first two draw their illustrations from and make reference specifically to the American church-growth scene. However, their basic transferable concepts are quickly evident and apply to almost any local church in almost any country.

Wagner, C. Peter. *Your Church Can Grow.* The best one-volume presentation of current church-growth concepts.

McGavran, Donald A., and Arn, Win. *How to Grow a Church.* Readable interview format, especially good on basics, classes of leaders, and church types with their problems and potential.

Gerber, Vergil. *God's Way to Keep a Church Going and Growing.* Good on New Testament church growth and very helpful on graphing.

McGavran, Donald A. *Understanding Church Growth.* Paperback or hardback. Written from the viewpoint of global church growth, with both local church and world church concerns. Excellent emphasis on cross-cultural church-growth principles which can be applied to the developing of ethnic ministries.

—PAUL R. ORJALA

About the Author . . .

Dr. Paul R. Orjala is professor of missions at Nazarene Theological Seminary, Kansas City, Mo. He was a missionary to Haiti under the General Board of the Church of the Nazarene. His academic training includes: A.B., Pasadena College, 1947; B.D., Nazarene Theological Seminary, 1950; M.A., Kennedy School of Missions, Hartford Seminary Foundation, 1956; Ph.D., Hartford Seminary Foundation, 1970.

1

God Wants
Your Church to Grow

God wants your church to grow! God wants every church to grow! So how come some do, some don't?

Come with me to Colorado Springs Eastborough Church of the Nazarene, perched close to Pikes Peak on the road to the Rockies . . . or to Pasadena First Church, in sunny California near the Pacific . . . or West Carrollton, Ohio, First Church, in the hearty midlands . . . or New Milford, N.J., in a state where there are more people per square mile than anywhere else in America.

What will you find at all these places?

You will find the exciting atmosphere of a growing church!

Before they even tell you, you sense the presence of new Christians, thrilled to find Christ, growing in grace and projecting the joy of new love.

And you will find mature Christians happily engaged in a ministry that matches their gifts. You will find worshipers submerged in a sense of God's presence and power.

13

None of these things are exclusive. Every church can have new converts, growing disciples, and God's presence. Dr. Raymond W. Hurn, executive director of the Department of Home Missions, reminds us that every church can grow "if there are people."

The four churches just mentioned are not as unusual as you might think. They were taken from a list of 600 growing churches selected from a computer study of growing Nazarene churches.

Of 600 growing churches studied, those shown below are a cross-section of rural, small city, and metropolitan churches in the Church of the Nazarene.

	Numeric Gain 1965-75	Decadal Growth Rate	1976 Membership
Colorado Springs Eastborough	419	855%	481
Pinellas Park, Fla.	109	681%	158
Hendersonville, Tenn.	78	520%	105
Denver, Colo., First	840	243%	1,323
Red Oak, Ia.	64	582%	86
Olathe, Kans.	528	866%	680
West Carrollton, Ohio	160	516%	194
Kingswood, W.Va.	71	789%	85
Salem, Ore., First	568	161%	997
Bloomington, Calif.	316	175%	498
Point Township, Ind.	45	900%	50
Pasadena, Calif., First	818	115%	1,568
Richardson, Tex.	260	1,182%	314
New Milford, N.J.*	131	935%	145

*Five-year study of 1970-75

God wants your church to grow in ways that fit your people and your community. As we study church growth, let's learn together from the best patterns of growing churches in rural communities, in small cities, and in

14

metropolitan areas. Let's examine workable ideas for older churches, new churches, small churches, and large churches, and those who may have plateaued at some point in their growth pattern.

Jesus said, "I will build my church" (Matt. 16:18). Augustine reminds us that without God, we *cannot;* but without us, God *will not.* Somewhere, we fit importantly into the picture.

What Is Church Growth?

In Matt. 28:19, Jesus told us our mission: *To make disciples of all nations.* Read and compare some of the modern versions of Scripture to settle this point firmly in your mind. It is the starting point for all that we will say and do regarding church growth.

Church growth, pure and simple, is the growth of the church by making disciples. Making disciples involves:

1. Helping people to receive Jesus Christ as their Lord and Savior;
2. Bringing them into the fellowship of the church;
3. Nurturing, training, and supporting them until they become ministering members of the Body of Christ.

In order to make more disciples, we must expand the organization of the local church and plant more congregations which can become centers of more church growth.

New Testament Church Growth

The Early Christian Church literally exploded upon the Mediterranean world. Jesus started with 12 disciples. Many modern-day churches start with more charter members than that! By the day of Pentecost, the number of loyal disciples had risen to "about" 120 (Acts 1:15) who were filled with the Holy Spirit in the Upper Room. They

15

were prepared for the fantastic growth which they were to see by prayer, obedience to God's Word, commitment to Christ, and the power of the Holy Spirit. Genuine church growth is not possible without this kind of preparation. We can never manipulate church growth. It takes the supernatural power of God in a miracle every time a person is converted. That is the only way that real church growth can take place. To see rapid church growth, we must be the people that God can use.

The church-growth story of Acts continues with the evangelism explosion on the Day of Pentecost when approximately 3,000 were added to the Church on the same day (Acts 2:41). But the growth didn't stop there. The report continues, telling us that "the Lord added to the church daily such as should be saved" (Acts 2:47). The number of believers soon reached 5,000 men (Acts 4:4). Then someone realized that they had neglected to count the women. The total was so great by this time that the record simply states "there were multitudes both of men and women" (Acts 5:14).

Up to this time, the Bible says that believers were *added* to the Lord, but soon an even more accelerated stage of growth is announced: "The number of the disciples was *multiplied*" (Acts 6:1, 7). At this point, persecution scattered the Christians except for the apostles (Acts 8:1), and the believers started the church-planting stage resulting in *church multiplication* (Acts 9:31). They moved out from Jerusalem to Judea, Samaria, and the ends of the earth (Acts 1:8). Within just a few years such great church growth had taken place that it is simply stated that there were tens of thousands of Christians (Acts 21:20).

Look at Your Church

Does all of this boggle your mind? Starting from one

original congregation! "It could never happen to us," you say? But it *could*—and it has happened hundreds of times in the history of the growth of the church since Pentecost. And something like this, to one degree or another, *must* happen if the millions (even billions on the world scene) who are without Christ are to be reached in our generation.

Now let's stop for a minute to see where *we* start—where *you* start in your own local congregation. Let's not be overwhelmed by the thought of unrealistic goals and huge numbers. Not every church and community has the same growth potential, but there is some way that your church can grow and fulfill God's plan for your congregation. A growth pattern sometimes develops slowly. Growth will come when God's people have the right vision, commit themselves to the right tasks, and are not afraid to work for the goals God gives them.

Let's take a look at *your* church. Let's rediscover your motive for growth. There are a lot of good things happening in your church. Stop for a minute and write them down on a sheet of paper. Now let's do some "imagineering." Look over the list and think how God could use these good things to help you discover opportunities for church growth in your own community.

Two Kinds of Growth

Some people want to debate the issue as to whether *qualitative* or *quantitative* growth is more important. The truth of the matter is that we need both kinds of growth. We need to "grow in grace and in the knowledge of our Lord and Saviour Jesus Christ" (2 Pet. 3:18). We also need to grow numerically as the Early Church did, as God prospered and blessed them. Numbers represent people, and we must learn to use *accountability through numbers* to make sure we are doing our best to minister to people

17

and build the kingdom of God. We must also choose methods of growth that will result in *sustained growth.*

Can Every Church Grow?

Three-fourths of Nazarene churches are located in nonmetropolitan areas. Can they grow also? The record of growing churches reveals that nonmetro churches can and do grow; and, as they grow, they send a steady stream of members into the cities in search of education or employment. There is also a growing trend of migration to nonmetro areas. Recent church growth in Soldotna, Alaska; Point Township, Ind.; and Red Oak, Ia., give abundant supporting testimony.

True enough, cities with thousands or millions of people may seem on the surface to be more promising for growth than rural communities. But don't overlook the possibility of quickly "cornering" the market in a rural area where a loving, caring, giving ministry gets attention rapidly.

Grand Coulee, Wash., Church of the Nazarene is a case in point. Nine years ago, about 20 persons worshipped in insignificant surroundings. Today, about 175 meet on Sunday in new, commodious facilities. The church has a constantly expanding witness for Christ. Lives are being changed at every level of community life, and in 1977 a new church was mothered by the Grand Coulee congregation in Bridgeport, Wash., about 40 miles away. Grand Coulee membership in 1977 was 90, or a 374 percent gain in 10 years.

Pastor Ron Hunter is the energetic, growing pastor at Grand Coulee. He testifies to the value of the longer pastorate for the development of a growing church in nonmetro. "You need to know your people, your community well," he says, "and let them get to know you. God works through men and it takes time."

Don't give up too quickly on the possibilities of growth. Even a sparse or declining population may still have many responsive and neglected people who can be reached. In a seemingly overchurched population, there are likely to be large numbers of "nominals" who need to be brought to a personal experience of Christ. These people will often know the language of the Bible and will understand the plan of salvation, especially when presented in the pattern of Evangelism Explosion, which speaks primarily to those of evangelical background.

Varieties of Growth and Loss

There are three sources of growth and three corresponding kinds of loss which are reported in church statistics:

Growth	Loss
1. Biological growth (from members' children)	1. Loss by death
2. Transfer growth	2. Transfer loss
3. Convert growth (by profession of faith)	3. Loss by removal

There is obviously nothing we can do about *loss by death* except to make the occasion of that loss a time of effective ministry to the bereaved.

Transfer loss and *transfer growth* are usually so near to being equal that they cancel each other out. However, in the case of population migration, the picture of church growth can be distorted if transfers in and transfers out are not taken into consideration in the interpretation of the statistics. Churches in some areas are doing an excellent job of evangelism, but lose many of their members when migration takes them to centers of population growth. Cities are generally such population-growth centers, but in the U.S. the trend has recently reversed in favor of rural areas near the cities. Churches in population-growth centers could show an abnormally high growth rate, principally due to transfers in, but that will not be automatic.

Evangelical churches often show transfer growth in from liberal churches when people are looking for a Bible-believing church with spiritual life. In receiving transfer members, it is important that they be acculturated to the doctrine and polity of the church and assimilated through friendship and opportunities for service.

Many churches lose approximately 50 percent of their convert growth by *removal*. The reasons are unique in each case, but five common causes are:

1. Spiritual regression—turning away from the gospel
2. Inadequate follow-up after conversion to disciple them
3. Failure to involve them in ministry in the church
4. Failure to involve them in satisfying friendship/fellowship relationships
5. Mismatch in socioeconomic class identification

If your church can reduce the percentage of those lost by removal, this will save individuals who might needlessly drift away from Christ and the church.

Biological growth (from members' children in the church) was in the past a significant avenue of growth. This is changing now due to smaller families and migration of children away from the home community. Our children, brought up in the church, are one of the church's most valuable resources for leadership and ministry. We all want to see our own children won for Christ. In most churches this is still thought to be the primary source of growth. If we take a 25 percent decadal growth rate for the

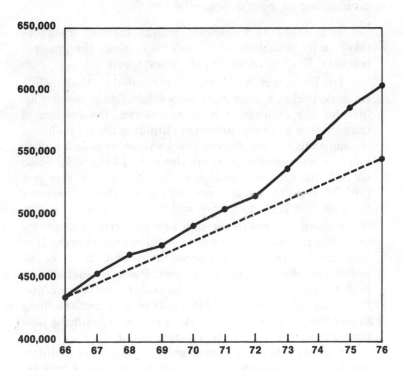

World Membership Growth
Church of the Nazarene
1966-1976

Total Membership Growth 38%

Biological Growth 25%

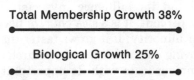

Note: Membership growth within the United States, Canada, and Great Britain was 28%.

general population as a rule of thumb, then the church that grows by only 25 percent per decade is only winning its own children—plus some convert growth to make up for children lost to the church. Hence it is a *static church,* neither increasing nor decreasing its percentage of the population and its influence in society. If it grows by less than 25 percent, it is a *sick church,* becoming a smaller and smaller minority. If it grows faster than 25 percent, it is an improving church. A healthy church is one which has growth commensurate with its opportunity, one which is maximizing its growth potential.

That leads us to *convert growth* through members taken in by profession of faith. This is where the greatest potential lies for increasing the growth rate.

Dr. Raymond W. Hurn has reminded us that "while we once told ourselves that we were building new buildings for our children and grandchildren, the realism of today makes us know that we are building the local church for someone else's children. Our own children and grandchildren will move somewhere else in all likelihood." Then we will have reason to thank God if someone else was faithful to plant and nurture the church that will receive our own children where they will live.

Expansion growth through new converts becomes for us a dire necessity if we are to survive as a church. It is here that the real vision, commitment, and ability of the pastor and church come to the test. Peter Wagner says in *How to Grow a Church* that "the *indispensible condition for a growing church is that it wants to grow and is willing to pay the price for growth.*" Both the pastor and the people must be involved in this commitment.

How fast should a church grow? The answer is different for every country, every location, and every population group accessible to a local church. The church that wants to *maximize its growth potential* and doesn't know what it is, can identify the fastest growing churches in its community and compare their growth rates. This will give it a base to start from. Responsiveness can also change very rapidly from one year to the next, increasing and decreasing.

Peter Wagner, who considers the United States to be a country responsive to the gospel at present, suggests the following rule of thumb for evaluation of growth in the U.S. by decade:

25% per decade	Poor growth in the U.S.
50% per decade	Fair
100% per decade	Good
200% per decade	Excellent
300% per decade	Outstanding
500% per decade	Incredible

The Scope of Church Growth

A few years ago, Ralph Winter of the School of World Mission, Pasadena, Calif., suggested a typology of the scope of church growth which has become widespread in its usage. He suggested four areas in which growth operates in the activities of the church.

1. *Internal* growth is the development of qualitative growth within the church, sometimes referred to as *nurture*. This involves doctrinal teaching and formation of ethical and spiritual patterns of life, and is the starting point for all other forms of church growth. Without internal growth, the church cannot be the Church.

2. *Expansion* growth is the numerical growth of the local church as new converts are won and incorporated into the church. This involves winning your own kind of people from the surrounding unchristian society.

3. *Extension* growth refers to the *planting of new churches* in the same society as the original churches.

23

4. *Bridging* growth is characterized by the planting of churches across a cultural barrier. This is typical missionary work, whether home missions among people of a contrasting culture, or world missions abroad. The name refers to "bridging" across cultures.

The Church-Growth Survey

There are three things you need to know about your local church which can be discovered through a church-growth survey: (1) the growth history of your church; (2) present strengths and weaknesses, and (3) the opportunities for growth that exist in the community. The church-growth survey is really three surveys: a statistical analysis, an organizational analysis, and a community analysis.

1. *The Statistical Analysis*

Chart on graph paper how the *membership* of the church has grown. A 10-year statistical analysis is long enough to indicate current trends. This requires 11 years of statistics so we can compute percentages of growth for the decade as well as for each year. The percentage of increase (or loss) is a more important index of growth than the number of new members because it can be used for comparison. Each year the percentage of growth should be calculated and compared with the preceding year's to see how well the church is growing.

We can see immediately that not all the growth has been at the same rate. There may even be some years in which there was a loss. The question is, *why* was there better growth one year than another? In order to find the answers, we'll have to dip into the history of the church. Check any existing records to pinpoint any changes that took place. Note time of pastoral change, new building opened, new parking lots, etc. Don't settle for superficial answers. Keep digging to find the causes of growth or loss.

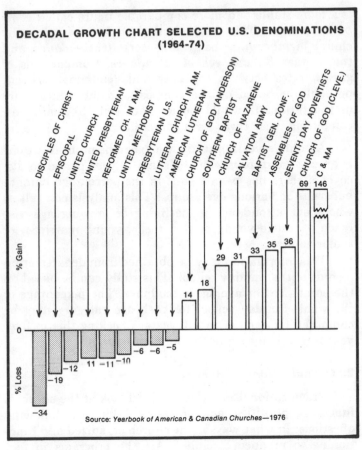

DECADAL GROWTH CHART SELECTED U.S. DENOMINATIONS
(1964-74)

Source: *Yearbook of American & Canadian Churches*—1976

On a separate graph, show the 10-year membership growth, adding a line graph indicating the biological growth at a rule-of-thumb percentage of 25 percent per decade. This indicates at a glance whether or not we have kept up with the proposed minimum of 25 percent biological growth for the decade.

Church growth experts are now using what they feel

25

is a more stable and more comparable figure called *composite growth*. This figure is derived by averaging the church *membership*, the average *worship attendance*, and the average *Sunday school attendance*. Comparisons of growth rates between churches and denominations will probably be based on the composite membership figure in the future. It would be advantageous to begin now computing these three for a composite.

Another revealing study which can be profitably done is an *age-group profile* of the same 10-year period to discover if there has been a shift in the percentage balance between the various age groups. This analysis can tell us where our attendance is declining or growing age-wise (such as single young adults, teens, young marrieds, or senior adults).

This information may be obtained from departmental records of the Sunday school. This study can be based on the enrollment or average attendance. The percentage of the whole Sunday school for each age category may be computed for each of the 10 years. Checking this in five-year intervals may quickly pinpoint certain trends.

2. *Organizational Analysis*

Organizational analysis is a hard look at the church's functions, priorities, and programs, asking the following questions: In what ways is the church organized and functioning to produce disciples? Are the programs in fact producing disciples? What needs to be changed so the church can produce more disciples? How many persons are involved in maintenance (teaching, administration, ushering, singing, serving on boards and committees, running auxiliaries, etc.)? How many are involved in work directly affecting the winning and discipling of new people? Chapters 3 and 4 will deal more directly with this area.

Areas that need to be investigated are: (1) The functioning of the structure and leadership personnel of the church; (2) the departments and auxiliaries of the church and their programs; and (3) the functioning of the facilities for church growth.

3. *Community Analysis*

Some surveys reveal that a local church is most effective in winning persons who live within a 12-minute travel radius from the church. Great care should go into analysis of the surrounding community. Good sources for community analysis may be obtained from Chambers of Commerce, state employment security offices, county planning commissions, and school districts.

CAPC (Census Access for Planning in the Church) provides a detailed breakdown of demographic characteristics for every census tract.* Computer programs have been developed which provide the census data most generally useful for church planning. Special adaptations can be made for slight additional cost.

Any church or district agency wishing to take advantage of the vast amount of research already done about a particular area should outline that area on a roadmap and send it along with a letter of inquiry to the Department of Home Missions, Church of the Nazarene, 6401 The Paseo, Kansas City, Mo. 64131.

---

*CAPC is an organization of church bodies designed to take advantage of United States Census data for church planning. The Church of the Nazarene is an associate member of this group and therefore Nazarene churches may utilize its services for a small fee.

CAPC has established a comprehensive library of computer tapes of data gathered by the United States Census Bureau. These tapes contain far more data than is available on printed reports.

The computer has the capability of breaking out this information for specific census tracts of concern to a particular local church, thus saving many hours of sifting through various printed reports.

You will receive a reply along with an estimate of the cost to you of such a program (minimum $50.00).

Census data can suggest possibilities for ministry. It can help you identify mission fields at home. It can tell you what groups are likely to have special needs.

Census data provides a picture at a specific point in time. Data now available was collected in 1970. Comparison with current estimates often available from Chambers of Commerce can identify trends in population growth, economic change, ethnic change, and so forth.

Canadian pastors have access to a wealth of demographic material closely resembling the CAPC breakdown through Statistics Canada. The address is as follows:

Statistics Canada
User Advisory Services
Data Dissemination
Ottawa, Canada
K1S 5A4

The Canadian census is conducted each five years and thus offers somewhat more current data than does the United States census, especially when the U.S. is nearing the end of a 10-year span. Beginning in 1980, the U.S. census will be conducted every five years.

Pastors in the United Kingdom can obtain census information through the following Government Bookshops:

49 High Holborn, London WC1V 6HB
13a Castle Street, Edinburgh EH2 3AR
41 The Hayes, Cardiff CF1 1JW
Brazennose Street, Manchester M60 8AS
Southey House, Wine Street, Bristol BS1 2BQ
258 Broad Street, Birmingham B1 2HE
80 Chichester Street, Belfast BT1 4JY

Why bother with all this detail and work? Because we are accountable—to God, to each other, and to the unsaved. Like the people in the parables of the talents (Matt. 25:14-30) and of the pounds (Luke 19:12-26), we are responsible for the abilities and advantages we have had. We must put them to use—God's use—in harvesting the people whose hearts God has prepared.

ACTION STEPS

1. *Something to Discuss*

a. Discuss the purpose of the church in the light of Matt. 28:18-20. What do we mean when we say that the goal of church growth is making disciples?

b. Trace the growth of the New Testament church in the Book of Acts. What were some of the disadvantages of the first Christians and what are some of the advantages we have now that they did not have?

c. Which is more important to the growth of the church, biological growth or convert (profession of faith) growth? In what way is this changing?

d. Consider the scope of church growth. What potential does your church have for expansion growth, bridging growth, extension growth?

2. *Something to Do*

a. Form a small Church Growth Committee to do research and prepare other data.

b. Identify the churches that are having outstanding growth. Get statistical data from these churches. Interview them as to the reasons for growth. What can be learned from each?

3. *Something to Read*

Gerber, Vergil. *God's Way to Keep a Church Going and Growing.* Growth in Acts, pp. 13-22; statistical analysis, pp. 45-74.

Jones, Ezra E. *Strategies for New Churches.* Community survey, information needed, pp. 58-76.

McGavran, Donald A., and Arn, Win. *How to Grow a Church.* Measuring church growth, pp. 57-75.

Parrott, Leslie. *Building Today's Church.* Church growth self-study, including finance, pp. 207-18.

Smith, Ebbie C. *A Manual for Church Growth Surveys.* Technical information for surveys at home and abroad.

Wagner, C. Peter. *Your Church Can Grow.* Composite membership and biological growth, pp. 62-64; growth in Acts, pp. 166-69.

(All these books are available through the Nazarene Publishing House.)

2

God's Gifts Will Help You Grow

Inasmuch as God through Scripture has revealed His desire for the discipling of all nations, He has also through Scripture promised enabling gifts to accomplish that desire.

The discovery of one's spiritual gifts gives each Christian his spiritual job description. Every Christian has at least one gift, a gift which establishes his area of ministry in the Body of Christ. Often the Holy Spirit gives individuals clusters of spiritual gifts in which one is primary and the others are supportive. St. Paul was a multi-gifted person with the capacity for several kinds of ministry.

The apostle Paul tells us in 1 Cor. 12:29-30 that there is no one particular gift that every Christian is supposed to have. Each one of us can find deep satisfaction in the gifts and ministry that God has given us.

Spiritual gifts must be placed in their proper setting within the Body Life concept. The Church is the Body of Christ—He is the Head and we are the members (Romans

12 and 1 Corinthians 12). Each member has his own function and each member is needed for the good of the whole Body. "We really do need each other," as Reuben Welch says in the title of his book.

Body Life finds its expression in *koinonia,* or the fellowship relationships of the church, and in mutual ministry. Koinonia is God's love in action between His people and produces the atmosphere described by such words as unity, mutuality, belonging, warmth, caring, sharing, commitment to each other, family feeling, appreciation, and affirmation. It builds a climate for church growth. Once a person has tasted it, he wants to be a part of it. In this functioning Body, spiritual gifts allow Christians to minister to each other and to the world.

This emphasis can produce a healthy church in which everyone finds his or her ministry and in which there are people to do all the tasks that are needed. Far from being a subject to be afraid of, a careful, biblical understanding of spiritual gifts is our best hedge against fanaticism and religious exhibitionism. Dr. W. T. Purkiser's book *The Gifts of the Spirit* is one of the best on this subject.

The Lists of Spiritual Gifts

After eliminating duplications, we have three lists related to spiritual gifts. We shall use Dr. Purkiser's terms for these gifts, which closely follow the language of the *New International Version* (NIV) of the Bible.

The Romans list (12:6-8) is often identified as the *primary gifts:*
1. Prophesying, or proclaiming God's Word
2. Serving, or helping
3. Teaching
4. Encouraging, or exhorting
5. Contributing to the needs of others, or giving

6. Leadership, or administration

7. Compassion, or showing mercy

Most interpreters agree that these seven primary gifts represent all the essential types of ministry that are needed in the local church and are at least potentially present in one degree or another in every church as a body of believers.

The list from 1 Corinthians (12:8-10) majors on *secondary gifts* "that are more exceptional, more transitory, less universal," according to Dr. Purkiser, possibly given for specific instances and not necessarily repeated:

1. Ability to speak with wisdom
2. Ability to speak with knowledge
3. Faith, or achieving faith, mustard-seed faith
4. Gifts of healings, to discern and believe when God wants to heal
5. Miraculous powers
6. Ability to distinguish between spirits
7. Different kinds of languages
8. Interpretation of languages

The church could exist without these, but God knows when they are appropriate to certain times, occasions, or situations.

The Ephesians list (4:11) names five offices or ministries which involve gifts for their functioning:

1. Apostles
2. Prophets
3. Evangelists
4. Pastors
5. Teachers

There is a gift of prophecy to equip prophets for their ministry of proclaiming the Word, and a gift of teaching for teachers. By analogy, it is assumed that there is a gift of apostleship for apostles, of evangelism for evangelists, and of pastoring for pastors.

Seek the Giver, Not the Gift

We are not to seek the gift but the Giver, the Holy Spirit. When we have Him and He has us, the question will be one of *discovering* the gift or gifts which He gives us for the edification of the Body. Apart from Him, the natural talent may remain, but the spiritual gift vanishes.

We may covet earnestly the best gifts. Paul recommends prophecy (1 Cor. 14:5)—and yet there is "a more excellent way," the way of love (1 Cor. 12:31 and all of chapter 13). Without God's sanctifying love in our hearts, gifts can be a snare. Gifts must have love to help them function in the Body for edification.

Discovering Your Gifts

Spiritual gifts are not identical with natural talents, though they may be related to them. Even in consecrated Christians, some developed natural abilities are unused by God, while other talents unknown or undeveloped suddenly spring into prominence as one's primary contribution to the Body.

How may we discover our gift or gifts? Peter Wagner gives five practical steps, as we keep the Romans list of primary gifts in mind:

1. Explore the possibilities
2. Experiment with as many as possible
3. Examine your feelings (what you like or enjoy doing)
4. Evaluate your effectiveness
5. Expect confirmation from the Body

And we might add a sixth step of inner confirmation by God's Spirit. Once we are assured about what our spiritual gift or gifts are, we are responsible for developing them and putting them to use.

34

How Gifts Are Used in a Local Church

In the First Church of the Nazarene in Roseburg, Ore., Pastor Everett Baker and his people have set up a program in which all new converts are led to the discovery of their spiritual gifts, helped to develop them, and given a place of service within the following possibilities:

Gift	Roles in the Church
1. Prophecy	Preachers, evangelists, teachers
2. Service	All kinds of work
3. Teaching	Researcher, teacher
4. Exhortation	Counselors
5. Giving	Finance committee
6. Administration	Committees
7. Mercy	Visitation

Such a program does not lead to regimentation but brings joy at the discovery of one's area of ministry for the Lord and for the Body. The result in the church is the growth that God gives, both in spiritual grace and in numbers. Who wouldn't want to attend a church like that?

The Relation of Gift and Role

In addition to the gift or gifts which the Holy Spirit has given each one as his special contribution to the functioning of the Body, *every* Christian has a *role responsibility* in the other areas. The one with the gift of teaching must also be ready to "preach, pray, or die at a moment's notice." He must be ready as well to serve, to encourage, to contribute, to lead, and to have compassion—to the extent of his ability. But these other areas are not where his primary ministry is to be found.

What is true of the primary gifts of Romans is also true of the leadership gifts of Ephesians 3. *Some* people do have the *gift* of evangelist. They have unusual ability and success in leading people to Christ. But not *every* Christian has this gift. Too long we have been heaping false guilt on ourselves by declaring or intimating that every Christian who is really Spirit-filled should be winning souls like a professional. Those of us who *can,* find it easy to criticize people who can't. However, *every* Christian has the *role* of witness—which on occasion results in people finding the Lord. Every Christian needs to volunteer for evangelism training to find out if he has the *gift* of evangelist, and if not, to help him better fulfill his *role* of witness so that he knows how to lead someone to Christ when the occasion arises.

Peter Wagner has a hypothesis that "in the average evangelical church, 10 percent of the members have been given the gift of evangelist" but that "of the 10 percent to whom God has given the gift of evangelist, only about one half of one percent are actively using it." This could be because they have not discovered their gift, because they are untrained, or because they have no channel to use it.

Leadership Gifts

The Ephesian list indicates that Christ has given to the *church* some as apostles, some as prophets, some as evangelists, and some as pastors and teachers "to *equip the saints for the work of the ministry.*" It becomes the responsibility of these leaders to discover the members of the church who have the gift of evangelist and are not using it, to train them, and to give them opportunity to use it. Any church that does this will have fantastic initial growth. If it wants to keep that growth, it will also have to help the other 90 percent to discover their spiritual gifts, train them, and give them opportunity to employ them in the edification of the whole Body.

There are three functional levels of ministry in the church:

1. *Role ministries,* which are the same for all Christians as part of their role as Christians;
2. *Body Life ministries,* in which there is specialization through spiritual gifts;
3. *Leadership ministries,* in which there is further specialization through leadership gifts.

Balance of Leadership Ministries

Dr. Donald McGavran has suggested the classes of leaders that are needed in the right proportion if denominations and local churches are to grow.

Class One leaders serve inside the church—church officers, board members, Sunday school teachers, choir members, committee members, and others.

Class Two leaders are volunteer workers who serve outside the church in outreach ministries to non-Christians in visitation evangelism and personal evangelism. They may at the same time double as Class One leaders.

Class Three leaders are leaders of small groups. They may be volunteers or partially paid, and they serve as leaders of Bible study groups, task force ministries to special groups, house churches, and the like.

Class Four leaders are the full-time, paid leaders of congregations, such as pastors and full-time staff members.

Class Five leaders are the superintending and motivating leaders who travel beyond the local church, such as district and denominational leaders.

All five of these classes of leaders are needed. They all contribute in one way or another to church growth. But if the proportion of Class Two leaders (outreach) is as small as that of Class Four leaders (paid professionals, e.g. pastors), there will be relatively little growth. The ideal balance between these classes of leaders for growth

Classes of Leaders

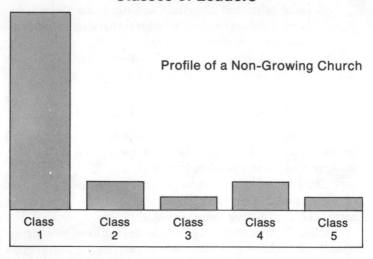

Profile of a Non-Growing Church

Class 1   Class 2   Class 3   Class 4   Class 5

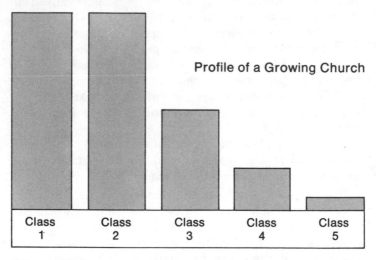

Profile of a Growing Church

Class 1   Class 2   Class 3   Class 4   Class 5

would be to have as many Class Two leaders (outreach) as Class One leaders (maintainence ministries), and a larger number of Class Three leaders (small groups) than Class Four leaders (full-time pastors and staff). A denomination with this pattern of leadership has great potential for growth.

Not all the workers among the Class Two leaders will be expected to have the gift of evangelist. Some will be needed to exercise the gift of hospitality; others, the gift of administration or teacher to keep the evangelism program running smoothly; others will drive cars or keep records, entertain newcomers, etc.

The key fact to keep in mind is that God has not given the church a world-changing assignment and then left us to accomplish it on our own resources. It is up to us to discover and apply the gifts that God has given us for the accomplishment of His will. God has not failed us yet; He will not fail us now.

ACTION STEPS

1. *Something to Discuss*

   a. What are the points of strength and what are the points of weakness in the Body Life of your church? How can the weak points be strengthened?

   b. Break up into small groups of about eight persons. Read again the lists of spiritual gifts. Tell each other what you think might be the spiritual gifts of others in the group, and then see how that compares with the idea that each one has of his own spiritual gift or gifts. Take care not to let this be a put-down.

   c. Discuss who in the church might have the gift of evangelist, then what might be some practical steps to help increase the number of Class Two leaders in the church.

d. What are some of the tasks that your church now expects your pastor to do that some of the members of the church could take up as a ministry and thus free your pastor for other things? (Don't move in and take over without talking it over with your pastor.)

2. Something to Do

a. Appoint a committee to study how you can help the people of your church discover their spiritual gifts. Maybe your pastor or someone else can hold a workshop on *Spiritual Gifts and Church Growth.*

b. Appoint someone to discover the distribution of members among the five classes of leaders. How can we get more Class Two leaders in this church?

3. Something to Read

McGavran, Donald A., and Arn, Win. *How to Grow a Church,* pp. 77-97, leadership for growing churches.

Purkiser, W. T. *The Gifts of the Spirit.* The whole book (75 pages).

Stedman, Ray C. *Body Life,* 149 pages.

Wagner, C. Peter. *Your Church Can Grow,* pp. 55-68, the pastor as the church-growth leader; pp. 69-83, mobilizing lay leadership.

3

Setting Goals for Growth

God has put a fantastic potential for evangelism in every Christian. It is the knowledge of salvation. Like Peter, we too have the keys of the Kingdom. We can loose people from their sins by sharing the knowledge of salvation, or we can withhold it and leave them bound (Matt. 16:19).

The problem of evangelism is a problem of distribution—getting the Good News distributed from those who have it to those who don't. God has given us the resources to get it distributed: (1) His Spirit—the power of evangelism (Acts 1:8); (2) His words—the message of evangelism (Acts 2:4); (3) His boldness—the style of evangelism (Acts 4:31), and (4) His joy—the reward of evangelism (Acts 5: 41).

Church growth and evangelism are not the same thing, although they have the same goal. The relationship of church growth to evangelism is that church growth activities are designed to pull the evangelism potential out of the church and out of each Christian and make sure that evangelism happens so that the church can grow. Church-growth activities precede, accompany, and follow up evangelism so that its results are conserved, utilized, and multiplied.

The Priority of Evangelism

Evangelism is the one essential and irreplaceable element of the mission of the church, which is "to make disciples" (Matt. 28:18-19). The church is never more than one generation from extinction. It must evangelize or there will be no one to be involved in nurture and social concern. People cannot be nurtured into the kingdom of God. They must be evangelized. Social concern is necessary to the credibility of the gospel, but it does not necessarily produce disciples.

This last third of the twentieth century will be known in history as the period in which apostasy spread through the churches like wildfire. The chief reason many churches no longer practice evangelism is that they no longer believe that people are lost and need the Savior. The *uniqueness of Christ*—"no other name" (Acts 4:12)—has been traded off for *religious pluralism* (many ways of salvation). The *universality* of God's offer of salvation through Christ (all may be saved by faith in Jesus) has been replaced by *universalism* (all men will be saved, or are already saved). Consequently they have refocused or redefined evangelism as social action. They see no need for evangelizing people, but they talk about "evangelizing the structures of society." *Humanization* is the word they substitute for evangelism or equate with it.

The result of the evangelistic bankruptcy of the main-line churches is abundantly clear in their unprecedented losses in membership in the past decade, in the dwindling numbers of ministerial students in their seminaries, and in the tragic retrenchment of their missionary programs around the world. All this is happening at a time when evangelical growth rates are increasing and the enrollment of evangelical seminaries is at an all-time high.

A professor of a mainline Protestant seminary said to me several years ago, "My denomination has lost its capacity to fulfill its part in the Great Commission. It is up to evangelicals like you to win the world today." We still know the Savior. We still believe the message. We still know how to deliver it. We still have the resources. If people are going to find Christ today, *we* are the ones who are going to have to win them. Who knows but what we are "come to the kingdom for such a time as this?" (Esther 4:14).

The Goal of Evangelism Is to Make Disciples

Evangelism is at the heart of church growth. The truth is that there is no real church growth until someone is saved. Accessions by transfer are important for the individuals involved, but it is like taking money out of one pocket and putting it in another—it doesn't mean that there is more money. Evangelism is at the center of church growth.

The Great Commission says, "Go ye therefore, and teach all nations, baptizing . . . teaching" (Matt. 28:19). The first word translated "teach" is a strong word meaning "to make disciples" and is translated this way in most modern versions. Biblical evangelism has as its goal not just bringing people to a decision to receive Christ, not even just helping them come to a place of assurance of salvation, but actually getting them on the road to being disciples of Jesus, taking up their cross and following Him (Mark 8:34). We *are* interested in seeing *disciples* multi-

43

ply, but not at the expense of offering "cheap grace," as Bonhoeffer put it.

In addition, as Nazarenes, we are aware that full discipling goes even farther. We are concerned that people not only become established as new Christians, but that they also enter into the experience of God's sanctifying grace. Our discipling responsibility continues as we sense their readiness and help new converts enter the life of holiness. This goal must always be kept in mind.

The Method of Evangelism

The relationship between evangelistic *goal* and evangelistic *method* is an intimate one. There are three basic methods that are being promoted by various groups today: presence evangelism, proclamation evangelism, and persuasion evangelism. They are listed here from the weakest to the strongest, but all three are necessary to biblical evangelism.

1. Evangelizing through Christian *presence* is held by some to be the only viable form of Christian witness today —just to be there in the name of Jesus. It emphasizes living the gospel before speaking the gospel, sometimes described as "earning the right to witness." There are situations and times where this approach is appropriate as a beginning. However, it must be recognized that until we are verbally identified with Christ, our good lives or good works will not be a witness to Him but only to ourselves. *Witness begins with identification with Christ.* The truth about the role of our Christian presence in evangelism is that we had better live out the gospel we share or we will lose our credibility. We must test *presence* as an evangelistic approach by whether or not it produces disciples. We are forced to the conclusion that if we stop with presence, it is insufficient to produce disciples.

2. One step farther toward biblical evangelism is *proclamation*. This is the verbalizing of the gospel. Some people think that the proclamation of the gospel is enough. The speaker "lays it on 'em"—now *they* are responsible. He has done his duty. They can take it or leave it, but now they have heard the truth. Or have they? This is what I call *hit-and-run evangelism*. It is message-centered rather than person-centered. Is our goal to deliver the message or to make disciples? We can win an argument and lose a person. God's way is to help us speak the truth in love (Eph. 4:15).

The mildest form in which proclamation evangelism is practiced is in *dialog*. With emphasis on the autonomy of the individual and fear of the immorality of manipulation, some Christians feel we can go no farther than *earning the right to speak by listening* and then offer the gospel as another option in life for a person to consider. The timid approach that is suggested by dialog seldom results in making disciples. We have something to say to lost men and women, boys and girls. It is not our message —it is God's. We must not only learn to listen, we must also learn to speak the Word of God with boldness, like the first Christians (Acts 4:31).

3. Until *persuasion* is added to *presence* and *proclamation,* there are seldom evangelistic results in disciples being made. Persuasion is mentioned six times in Acts in referring to the style of Paul's ministry, and he owns it as his approach: "We persuade men" (2 Cor. 5:11). If we believe our gospel, and if we really love people, it makes a difference to us as to whether or not they come to know God's saving grace. We cannot be neutral about such an important possibility for their life. We do not believe we can get someone into the Kingdom through sheer force of our persuasion, but God can use loving persuasion to open a person's heart and move his will to decision and faith.

45

The Purpose Is to Win Souls

Growing churches plan to get people saved. They do not just hope they will and leave it to chance. They are not satisfied just to get people into the church as attenders. Their goal is first, foremost, and constantly to get new contacts converted. They do not wait until the next revival, but they seek by all means—personal evangelism and public evangelism—to lead them to Jesus.

If we intend to make disciples, we must be willing to pay whatever price is demanded of us. As a small child, our daughter Jeannie once asked, "Does Jesus have to stoop down to get into our hearts?"

What I first took for a childish imagination was suddenly turned into one of the most profound insights. "Yes, Jeannie," I replied. "Jesus does have to stoop down to get into our hearts."

That is what Philippians 2 is all about—Jesus leaving the honor and glory of heaven to stoop down and enter our world of sin and suffering, to share our experiences and identify with us in His redeeming death, and identify with us in His resurrection and exaltation. But the startling thing about that passage is that Paul says, "Let this mind be in you, which was also in Christ Jesus" (Phil. 2:5). Are we ready to become involved in other people's lives so that, as Jesus did for us, we may be used to make Him visible, credible, and available to those who need Him? That's what it takes to make disciples.

Philosophies of Evangelism

How should we evangelize? *Who* should be evangelized? and *When* should we evangelize? are the three most important questions of a philosophy of evangelism. In answering the question "How?" we shall look at the contrasting "Come" and "Go" philosophies. The issue of

46

"Who should be evangelized?" is found in selective versus inclusive evangelism. The concepts of responsiveness and resistance answer the "When?" question.

"Come" and "Go" Philosophies

The Bible uses both the words "come" and "go" in relation to mission and evangelism. *"Come"* refers to God's gracious invitation to salvation (Isa. 55:1; Matt. 11:28). The Church and all who hear are invited to join with the Spirit in this open invitation to God's grace (Rev. 22:17). This is the word of the Lord and the word of the Church to the world.

However, once we have come, God's word to His people is *"Go!"* After Isaiah responded, "Here am I; send me," the Lord said to him, "Go, and tell this people" (Isa. 6:8-9). And, of course, the starting point of the Great Commission is "Go!" (Matt. 28:19; Mark 16:15).

Those who *come* will find God's salvation, but what about those who will not come? They need to be saved too. So someone must *go* to them with the gospel that they may hear and believe.

It is here that Israel failed to get God's revelation to the nations, with only a come-strategy for the most part. But from the beginning, the New Israel—the Church— has had both a come-strategy and a go-strategy, and the gospel has been spread from Jerusalem to the ends of the earth.

There are many local churches like Israel that are hindered by having only a come-strategy for evangelism. Some come, but very few. *One of the big differences between growing churches and static churches is that growing churches have both come-structures and go-structures for evangelism and are using both to full advantage.*

What are *come-structures* in the local church? They

47

are special services, evangelistic meetings, concerts, special day programs, and activities that will draw new people into the church. They may be evangelistic in nature or not, but the church takes nothing for granted and matches these come-structures with *go-structures* that send their people out into the homes of these visitors to share the gospel with them. They thank the Lord for everyone who finds Him inside their church, but they go after those who do not respond in a public service and try to win them in personal contact while the impact of their visit is still fresh in their memory.

Gene Edwards says that it is easier to win a soul to Christ than it is to get him to come to church. James Kennedy says that it is easier to win someone to Christ who has visited your church than someone who has never been in your church. Who is right? They are both right, but they are talking about different people. Some people will come to church, hear the gospel, accept it in church or later at home when someone goes to them. Other people won't come to church under any circumstances, but they will respond to personal evangelism in their home when someone goes to them.

So we see the need for both come-structures and go-structures in the evangelistic program of the local church.

Selective Versus Inclusive Evangelism

Because it is easier to win someone to the Lord who is like us, our evangelism will probably turn out to be somewhat selective—we spend more time with our kind of people. But when the Lord brings people across our pathway who are members of other groups, it is often for the purpose of our witness to them. They may have no one else in their acquaintance who can share the gospel with them. If we would be obedient to our Lord, we dare not be deliberately selective in our evangelism.

Pagans have the least knowledge of the gospel, converted and growing church members the most. This means that if we do the easiest thing in witnessing, we'll work on the backsliders first, the nominal Christians second, and the pagans last. Which is exactly what most of us do. In a revival, most of the people who go to the altar are backsliders, a few nominals, and maybe one stray pagan. The backsliders know what the gospel is, the nominals know the language but haven't really understood it, and the pagans hardly understand our language.

Backsliders are important to bring back into the fold. They are worth the tender loving care it often takes to help them get reestablished in the Lord. But we cannot allow ourselves to be so occupied with them that we miss opportunities to lead others to Christ. Nominals constitute a huge number of people who think they are all right spiritually yet have never been born again. We must not assume that anyone around the church is automatically a Christian. We must ask the Lord to give us sensitivity that will help us identify those who are around but still on the outside spiritually and lead them to a personal knowledge of Christ. They are often responsive to the right approach.

But pagans—raw pagans! What do you do with them? They look like nice people and are hard to identify. This is where we must obey the gentle nudging of the Spirit when He indicates that we should witness to someone. But the ones that look like pagans and act like pagans—is there any use trying to get them to understand what the gospel is all about? We may have to learn how to talk to them in a dialect other than the language of Zion. It isn't easy at first to witness in everyday language! But it will be well worth it. Many unbelievers are sick of their sins but don't know any other way. Their hearts are ready to believe when someone cares enough to tell them.

The pluralistic assumption of many people today is that once a person identifies himself as of another faith, we should not try to share the gospel with him—that somehow it is impolite, an affront to him. In visitation evangelism, we used to ask people if they were Protestant, Catholic, or Jewish. If they said Catholic or Jewish, we crossed them off the list as unlikely contacts. If they said Protestant, we asked them what denomination, and if they said none, we figured it was open season on them.

This goes back to our motive for evangelism. If it is primarily to get more members for *our* church, it does smack of proselyting. But if it is first of all to help them find Christ, it is appropriate for us to evangelize anybody. Of course, we'll invite them to our church, and if they have found the Lord through us, they will be likely to come. They need not be coerced.

The ethclass fallacy is the suggestion that we probably couldn't win someone of another race or social class to the Lord, so why try? Whites, Blacks, other minorities, foreigners—let them each win their own. But what if there is no one available but you? A sincere witness empowered by the Holy Spirit can break through class and race barriers. Witnessing to people who are not like us is one way that we can show our love for them. Most of them will deeply appreciate it and some will find Christ. The foreigners who are in our midst, many of them students, are a strategic group that can take the gospel back to their country, some of them to places where missionaries cannot go.

Responsiveness and Resistance

Where do new converts come from? They come from the responsive segments of society. Then we must know which segments those are.

50

1. *The necessity of priorities* results from the fact that we do not have enough resources to concentrate on both the responsive and the resistant in equal measure, if we are to bring in the harvest of all those who are responsive at present. We do not have enough personnel, money, time, and facilities to do everything. The question then comes, what shall we do?

2. *Concentrate on the responsive* is the only reasonable strategy. We cannot base our strategy on need alone—it must be based on the needs of the responsive. This does not mean that we will ignore the resistant, but we will not multiply our efforts to win them until we see responsiveness beginning to develop. We will sow the seed, water it, and keep a watch for signs of change. We never know when someone or some group is going to become responsive, and will benefit from this strategy.

3. *When are people responsive?* They are most often responsive when others are moving toward the gospel. Don't be satisfied with just one person—try for the whole family, the whole group. Don't lose time; press the issue immediately. Train new Christians right away to win their families and friends.

People are responsive when leaders are accepting the gospel. They trust the judgment of people they admire and follow. Go out for the men and you'll get the group; for fathers, and you'll get the family. Don't be intimidated by people in leadership roles—they are often lonely, uncertain, and insecure. They long for love and concern.

People are responsive when change is taking place in their lives, in the community, or in the world at large. People are open when there is a change in personal relationships, such as when the last child leaves home, when there is a change in residence or work, or when retirement comes. People are open in times of personal crisis: death, divorce, financial trouble or other failure, loss of a job, accident, fire, sickness. People are also more open to the gospel at times of happy events that bring change, such as marriage, moving to a new location, birth of a child (especially the first), and at the time of honors or attainment. Whole communities may become responsive at times of natural disaster—flood, earthquake, tornado, epidemic, war. Communities become responsive also when there are social or cultural changes that they cannot handle—drugs, juvenile delinquency, rising crime rate, recession, problems with schools.

It is at times like these that Christians have a maximum opportunity to reach individuals and groups with a supportive ministry and an introduction to Jesus Christ.

Responsiveness is not an innate quality in persons or groups. It is related to events, conditions, social relationships, and the general directions of social change. Responsiveness can change to indifference or even hostility. That is why there is a priority to reaching those who are responsive, before they change in their attitude toward the gospel.

Resistance may change to responsiveness. Sometimes God creates readiness for the gospel in a more or less direct way, especially when He develops responsiveness in larger groups. Our responsibility is to discover what God is doing and then respond to His guidance. More often God uses us with individuals and small groups. We must not blame resistance merely on the people we are trying to reach—it may be due to our neglect. Attention and concern may turn resistance into responsiveness. Resistance may be due to our inadequate approach or failure to find the right points of contact. Cultural clues may help us gain access to their confidence.

When efforts to create readiness for the gospel fail, however, we must not heap false guilt on ourselves. Maybe it is a question of timing. Our efforts may bear fruit in

DISCIPLESHIP: THE TOTAL PROCESS

● **PHASE I: "Making Disciples"**

	Original Engel Scale
Stage 1—Ignorance of Christ (may be exposed, but pays no attention)	−10 / −9
Stage 2—Awareness of Christ (sees Christ as an option)	−8 / −7
Stage 3—Understanding of Christ (realizes what knowing Christ means)	−6 / −5
Stage 4—Personal involvement with Christ (recognizes what Christ could do for him)	−4 / −3
Stage 5—Decision (verdict) for Christ (I want or don't want Christ)	−2 / −1
Stage 6—Regeneration, conversion (disciple making—theologically)	0 / +1
Stage 7—Incorporation into body of Christ (disciple counted—strategically)	+2

● **PHASE II: "Training Disciples"**

Stage 8—Witnessing for Christ

+3 etc.

Adapted from James Engel and H. Wilbert Norton, *What's Gone Wrong with the Harvest?* p. 45. Copyright 1975 by Zondervan Publishing House. Used by permission.

the future. It is a time for continuing to sow the seed, water it, and wait in hope for the harvest. Meanwhile, our task should be that of testing to find out where there is responsiveness and turning to the harvest where it can be found.

The Evangelistic Program of Growing Churches

1. *Growing Churches Know Where Their Converts Come From*

Growing churches have tried many different methods, and they know which ones produce converts in their church and community and which ones do not. They can tell you how many people find the Lord at a public altar in their church and how many find the Lord through personal evangelism calls in the home. They know the relative success of evangelistic Bible-study groups, circles of concern, and bus ministries for winning new people. They know whether or not converts in their community can be won through the contacts of a day-care center or ministry to the handicapped.

They know whether people in their community respond better to the Kennedy method or to the Four Spiritual Laws. They know the best channels for public relations in their community and how people respond to special days, special programs, and concerts. They know how effective a channel the Sunday school is for evangelism. They know how many converts come from revivals.

A survey of growing Nazarene churches revealed that the public altar rated very high as an evangelistic method in winning converts. However, in a follow-up questionnaire, it was learned that "seldom" do people kneel at public altars who were not first carefully nurtured, instructed, or otherwise dealt with in terms of the plan of salvation. One single program of evangelism will not fit every church. Don't fear to innovate in your situation.

54

2. *Growing Churches Plan for Results*

Growing churches prepare for revival with the intention that there will be converts. Revival often starts in the prayer cells while people are praying for the coming revival. Growing churches get out attractive advance publicity, until their whole community knows there is going to be a revival. They plan in advance to invite unconverted friends and contacts to dinner and the revival services. They make every night of the revival a special event with a choir and crusade atmosphere. They make sure there are unconverted people in every service so there are real prospects. They have trained altar workers prepared to pray immediately with seekers when they come. They have follow-up literature and programs so they can start the new Christian out right the night he accepts the Lord.

The Department of Evangelism provides helpful materials on the philosophy and procedures for revivals. In addition, some important new books are now available on evangelism. Many Nazarenes are already using Charles (Chic) Shaver's *Basic Bible Studies for New Growing Christians.* His latest book, *Conserve the Converts,* goes directly to the vital issue of follow-up. Dr. Leslie Parrott has written a new book, *Renewing the Spirit of Revival,* which deals directly with the issue of revival, as does *The Revival Meeting in the Twentieth Century,* by Chuck Millhuff. All these resources are available from the Nazarene Publishing House.

3. *Growing Churches Train People for Evangelism*

They are actively looking for the 10 percent who have the gift of evangelist and training them for personal evangelism. They have people who are skilled in training others in evangelism, so the program can continue to expand. They use their evangelists in calling on contacts, such as visitors to their church, in fellowship evangelism in Christians' homes, and in evangelistic Bible studies. They have trained altar workers for public services and revivals. They have trained workers for follow-up Bible studies with new converts.

4. Growing Churches Incorporate New Converts into the Church

They tie new converts into the church immediately after they have accepted the Lord, often through a new converts' Sunday school class or church membership class. They help them discover their own spiritual gifts and develop them for use. They train new converts in evangelism immediately so they can utilize their contacts with their unconverted friends, associates, and family. They know that in six months to a year these contacts will have less potential than they have immediately after a person accepts the Lord.

5. Growing Churches Utilize Multiple Channels of Ministry

They develop programs so there is a way that every Christian can find a ministry, such as letter writing for shut-ins and senior adults; transporting senior adults for shopping and to church; ministries to the deaf, blind, and retarded; mothers' clubs; single adults; Christian business women's groups; and men's fellowships. They consciously integrate evangelism into all that the church does so as to maximize its evangelism potential.

6. Growing Churches Specialize in What Works Best for Them

Few churches try to do all of these things at once. Through trial and error they discover where and how they get the best results and concentrate on those programs. From time to time, as opportunity opens up or as the Lord specifically leads, they begin new evangelistic programs and sometimes phase old ones out. They are strictly pragmatic when it comes to expecting their programs to produce disciples. They feel this is a part of their stewardship of time and resources.

Evangelism Potential

Each one of us is an inside member of at least eight important homogeneous units (areas of influence). We identify with other people who are members of each unit, and they identify with us. We already have access to the communication system, credibility, and the ways of thinking of each group. We meet members of some of these groups daily and others from time to time.

Many of the members of these groups—in some cases, a majority—are not yet Christians. You may be the only born-again Christian that some of them know. God wants to reach these people. He can reach them through you. Are you ready to let God begin to engineer your circumstances so that you can share the gospel with some of them one by one? You won't be alone—Christ will be with you. You won't have to do it in your strength—you can do it in the power of the Holy Spirit. Church growth can begin with you.

Look at each homogeneous unit, or area of influence, in the diagram and make a rough estimate of how many people in each unit there are whom you know personally who are not yet Christians. The average person's total of all the groups is usually over 100. This is your EP (evangelism potential). Now calculate the EP of your church by multiplying the membership by 100. The total EP of your church is absolutely astounding.

EVANGELISM POTENTIAL
IN YOUR
AREAS OF INFLUENCE
(HOMOGENEOUS UNITS)

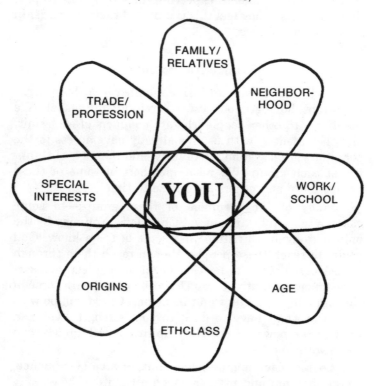

Now let's look for a place to begin. Start a prayer list with the name of one unconverted acquaintance of yours in each homogeneous unit—that will be eight names. Let's start praying for these people and ask God to open the door for us to witness to them in a natural, winsome way. Let us pray that God may prepare their hearts for our witness and that they may receive Christ as their Savior. Let's look for ways to get them into the church where they can receive more of God's Word and experience the fellowship of God's people. Let's continue in prayer and obedience until we begin to see some of these people come to the Lord and be saved.

ACTION STEPS

1. *Something to Discuss*

a. Describe the 3 "Ps" of evangelism.

b. How does each theological approach "affect" the making of disciples?

c. How do each of us fit into the process of evangelism?

d. What is included in an adequate follow-up of new converts?

2. *Something to Do*

a. Make an inventory of the "person hours" given to maintenance (worship, choir practice, teaching, ushering, board meetings, committee meetings, etc.) and compare it to an inventory of "person hours" spent in outreach. Is 10 percent of the total "person hours" of your church spent in personal evangelism?

b. What maintenance programs could be modified or even cancelled to give more time to evangelism?

c. Choose someone to study and report on the come-and go-structures of evangelism in your church. Draw up recommendations for your local Church Growth Committee to consider.

3. *Something to Read*

Edwards, Gene. *How to Have a Soul Winning Church.* Excellent concepts on go-structures of personal evangelism.

Engel, James, and Norton, H. Wilbert. *What's Gone Wrong with the Harvest?* pp. 31-42, audience orientation; pp. 43-58, making disciples and the Engel scale; pp. 59-78, proclamation, persuasion, and cultivation.

Gibson, Donald, compiler. *New Testament Evangelism.* Manual for training lay persons in personal evangelism, prayer cells, friendship evangelism, and church growth.

Kennedy, D. James. *Evangelism Explosion.* The Coral Ridge program for lay witness.

McDill, Wayne M. *Evangelism in a Tangled World.* Answers to problems in contemporary setting for mass and personal evangelism.

Millhuff, Chuck. *The Revival Meeting in the Twentieth Century.* How to prepare effectively for mass evangelism. Includes a checklist which is very practical in preparing before, during, and after revival.

Parrott, Leslie. *Renewing the Spirit of Revival.* Showing need of creating the atmosphere for spiritual renewal and the Holy Spirit's leadership to real revival.

Potter, Lyle. *Abundant Life.* Useful flip chart in presenting sanctification.

Shaver, Charles (Chic). *Conserve the Converts.* A study on follow-up.

Worrell, George. *How to Take the Worry Out of Witnessing.* Practical applications to youth on effective witnessing.

4

Targeting for Maximum Growth

The fisherman who knows how to catch fish doesn't just go out to catch "fish." He goes out prepared to catch a specific kind of fish. He knows that fish are not all alike in their habits. He knows where and when to find each variety. He knows which kind of bait or lure to use for each kind. He uses different sizes of hooks for different-sized fish and a different strength of line as well. Some varieties are caught on the bottom, others near the surface, some around rocks, and others around weeds. Some are caught by casting, some by trolling, others by net. If you ask the real fisherman how to catch fish, he will reply, "What kind of fish do you want to catch?" There is a different strategy for each kind of fish.

Church growth studies have taught us that if we want to be successful in winning people to Christ in larger numbers, we must find out what they are like, what groups they belong to, what motivates them, how they make their decisions, what their preferences are, what kind of person they will trust, what they believe, and how much they know about the gospel.

People are not just individuals floating around in society, but they are individuals who are members of groups. When we begin to see people in their webs of relationships, we begin to develop the potential for winning not just one individual in isolation, but often many in a chain reaction of mutual influence which God can use.

The Role of Culture

No church grows in a social vacuum. It grows in a given society and in a given community. That community is composed of groups of individuals who identify with others in their group on the basis of the life-style and values that they hold in common. That basis we call *culture;* it is called a *subculture* if it is a subvariety of a larger group. In small communities, there may be only one group and everyone is a part of it. In larger communities, there may be many groups with contrasting cultures or subcultures. People who share the same culture are constantly influencing each other. If we can get on the inside of that culture with the gospel, it can spread from person to person by way of the cultural communication networks that are already built in.

If it is our culture, we are already on the inside. We know the communication networks. We are already related to many, many people. It is easier to win people like ourselves because we already understand them and have credibility with them.

But if it is another culture that is involved, we are going to have to learn how to understand those people and how to interact with them, for the most part, on their own basis. St. Paul said, "I am made all things to all men, that I might by all means save some" (1 Cor. 9:22). Getting on the inside of someone else's culture can be one of the most exciting experiences of a lifetime. It becomes doubly exciting when it enables you to win them to Christ.

Homogeneous Units

Dr. McGavran invented a term that is useful for describing groups with which people identify. The contrasts between such groups may be very great or very small, but the principle of identification and influence is the same. The term is "homogeneous units," indicating groups of people who share a "sameness" at one or many points. The spread of the gospel has followed the lines of homogeneous units from the very beginning.

Let's look at the story in John 1:35-46. John the Baptist points out Jesus to two of his disciples, Andrew and John (as it is usually interpreted), who immediately follow Jesus. Andrew tells his brother Simon Peter that they have found the Messiah and brings him to Jesus. Jesus finds Philip, who is of the same city as Andrew and Peter, and calls him to follow. And Philip tells his acquaintance Nathanael about Christ.

This is quite a chain reaction! It starts first of all with the homogeneous unit of a *religious group,* John the Baptist and his disciples. Next, the witness travels through a *kinship* homogeneous unit, the brothers Andrew and Peter. Then a *locality* group is the focus—Andrew and Peter's credibility with Philip is used by Jesus. Finally a *friendship* group comes into play with Philip and Nathanael. The whole passage takes on a new light. And this kind of understanding is what McGavran calls *people consciousness.* Let us look at some of the types of homogeneous units that can form the basis of people consciousness.

1. *Biological:* race, age, sex, kinship
2. *Locality:* residence, origin, neighborhood, school or work location

63

3. *Cultural:* language, social class, nationality, ethnic
4. *Economic:* work/profession/trade (blue collar, professional, clerical, unemployed)
5. *Personal/social:* special interests (hobbies, sports, common experiences)

Homogeneous units function for a number of very important purposes:

1. Identity and belonging
2. Credibility and protection
3. Influence and control
4. As a communication network

When any of these functions can be captured for Christ, rapid church growth through the unit is possible. So-called mass movements, or, as McGavran prefers to call them, "multi-individual conversion patterns," take place more often than supposed, simply because they go unrecognized when they are in less spectacular numbers. This is what often happens during a revival.

The Bible is explicit about cultural diversity in the patterns of conversion. It identifies the origins of the people who heard the gospel on the day of Pentecost (Acts 2:7-11). At first, some of the Jewish Christians thought the Gentiles had to take on Jewish customs at the time they became Christians, but this was settled at the first Jerusalem council (Acts 15)—they could be Gentile Christians. Today we are finally realizing that Jews don't have to renounce their Jewishness in order to become Christians. We are seeing in our generation the first significant breakthrough in Jewish evangelism since the first century in the *Jews for Jesus* movement, and other such organizations.

The U.S. Mosaic

What does this mosaic of homogeneous units in a society look like? Let us take the United States for an example—though every country would show a similar system. There is a dominant cultural group plus many different minorities. The dominant cultural group in the U.S. is called WASP (White Anglo-Saxon Protestants). In the past, the U.S. followed a policy of trying to assimilate its new immigrants and make "Americans" out of them. The assimilation was to the WASP culture, which developed from the culture of the first immigrants. Enough immigrants have "melted" into this cultural group until it constitutes 56.6 percent of the U.S. population. This leaves 43.4 percent of "unmelted" ethnics.

Today, the U.S. has discovered that instead of having a "melting pot" where differences disappear, it has a "stew pot" in which each group flavors the others while still maintaining its own distinctive identity. This makes it all the more important that the gospel does not become the monopoly of one or two groups in a society, but that the gospel penetrates into every group so that it can grow and flourish inside all of them.

This is not an argument for segregation, but for the right of cultural identity and integrity. The right of integration must be advocated and upheld by the church, for the gospel has come to break down all walls of separation. However, many minorities today do not want to pay the price of assimilation for the privilege of integration. That is why they say "Black is beautiful" and "Brown is beautiful." The advantage of the gospel is that it can fit them as they are.

The major ethnic groups in the United States are the Blacks and the Spanish (or Hispanic), each with approximately 25 million. They, in turn, are composed of many groups that contrast in origin and other cultural characteristics. Unmelted ethnic Germans and Irish who still retain strong identity are the next two largest groups,

MIGRATION PATTERNS

Polynesians
Chinese
Japanese
Asians

Mexican, South and
Central Americans

Cubans

West Indies
Blacks

European
British

Puerto
Ricans

followed by smaller numbers of Italians, Polish, Russians, and others.

Groups of people in the U.S. contrast not only at the point of ethnic identity but also in social class. Putting these two concepts together, we come up with the term "ethclass," which is a useful way of referring to the total identity of every individual. *Social class* identity in the U.S. is determined by three components: *economic class*

THE STATE OF THE U.S. "MELTING POT"

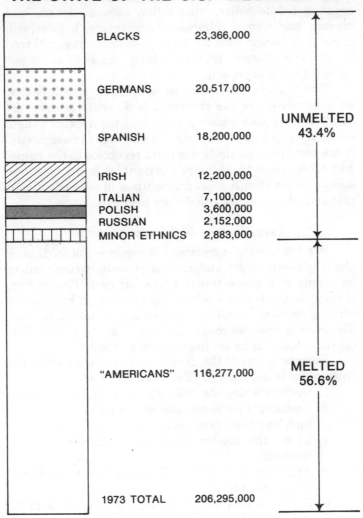

BLACKS	23,366,000	
GERMANS	20,517,000	
SPANISH	18,200,000	UNMELTED 43.4%
IRISH	12,200,000	
ITALIAN	7,100,000	
POLISH	3,600,000	
RUSSIAN	2,152,000	
MINOR ETHNICS	2,883,000	
"AMERICANS"	116,277,000	MELTED 56.6%
1973 TOTAL	206,295,000	

Source: Statistical Abstract of U.S. 1974
Adapted by Dr. C. Peter Wagner. Used by permission.

(rich, upper middle, middle, lower middle, low, and poor); *vocation* (white collar, blue collar, service workers, and others); and *formal schooling* (elementary, high school, or college). Information on these classifications is gathered by the U.S. Census Bureau, which can help us in our church-growth approach.

The importance of all this for church growth is that we must recognize the tremendous diversity represented by all of these homogeneous units and not approach them with the gospel as if they should all react the same way. Some homogeneous units are more *receptive* to the gospel and others seem to be more *resistant*. It is the receptive units that we should concentrate upon in evangelism and cultivate the resistant until they begin to respond.

Targeting for Maximum Growth

We are always targeting. If we are not conscious about who our target audience is, it usually turns out to be people with characteristics like our own. That is fine, if they are the ones we are trying to reach. If not, we are wasting our time by not making our target specific enough. The more specific we make our targeting, the more powerful the effect can be on that target audience.

Everybody needs the gospel, but communicating the truth alone is not enough. Targeting involves:

1. Distinguishing the different groups to be reached;
2. Learning their needs and interests;
3. Speaking their language;
4. Using the media through which they can be reached;
5. Appealing to proper motives that will bring acceptance from them;
6. Putting it all together so they can identify with it.

Even people who are "like us" can be broken down into smaller, more homogeneous, units for more direct targeting. We have been doing this for years in the church with regard to age-groups in Sunday school classes and youth groups. We need to extend this ability now to other homogeneous units that need to be reached more effectively with the gospel.

Targeting involves two features: (1) *range* and (2) *focus*. *Range* refers to how broad a target audience is that we are trying to reach. Our targeting range may be either *broad-spectrum* or *narrow-spectrum*. If we are trying to reach several homogeneous units at once, that is broad-spectrum targeting. If we are working on only one homogeneous unit, that is narrow-spectrum targeting.

Focus refers to how specific our communication is going to be. It may be a *single focus* communication, which would be normal for a narrow-spectrum target audience; or it may be a *multiple focus* communication, which is needed for a broad-spectrum target audience.

When we cannot choose our target audience and it includes a variety of people (broad spectrum), then we must use a multiple-focus communication style or we will exclude some groups from our communication. Preaching is generally directed to adults and automatically excludes children—no wonder they get fidgety or go to sleep. Speakers to predominately male audiences often forget there are women in the audience and speak to the men, often addressing them to the exclusion of the women.

We can target by our choice of the communication channel, such as in music. Anyone can take good classical church music once in a while, but a steady diet of it may prompt a blue-collar worker to move to another church. Youth outreach music is great for reaching teens, but is a little less successful in getting a message to senior adults. Actually, a balanced multiple-focus communication pattern will help everyone to expand his range of appreciation and give everyone something with which he can identify.

The key is to know your people and design your communication accordingly.

One of the most important questions we need to ask ourselves in our involvement in Christian communication is: Am I choosing my communication style and format to please myself, or to fit my audience? In evangelism, the targeting principle is extremely important. It often makes the difference as to whether someone will listen or turn deaf ears to the gospel.

The way in which a local church uses the targeting principle is one of the most important keys to the philosophy of ministry in that church. It decides whom they want and whom they don't want. Most churches sooner or later unconsciously become focused on one homogeneous unit. This is sometimes true of a whole denomination. The membership becomes oblivious to any who are different from their kind of people.

Targeting is a tool which can work for us or against us in church growth. The situation must be taken into consideration. When there is one segment of society that is particularly responsive, the church that directs its focus toward that homogeneous unit is going to have greater opportunity to win them. Provided that everyone is welcome in all the churches, it is not an unchristian thing for there to be several contrasting homogeneous unit churches of the same denomination in a city. If someone does not feel at home in one, he will feel at home in another which fits his *ethclass* (or ethnic and class identity). Such a specialization will facilitate church growth and ensure that all the groups within an area will have the best advantage to be reached. This is a strong argument for church planting on a broad scale.

Four Types of Evangelism

The spread of the gospel in Acts follows the outline of

the commandment of Jesus that the disciples should be witnesses in Jerusalem, Judea, Samaria, and the uttermost parts of the earth (Acts 1:8). In addition to the obvious geographical extension from a center, there is another important thing to be seen that is relevant to evangelism everywhere. The church-growth movement has systematized this pattern in a very useful way which highlights the different types of evangelism which need to be done by the church.

E-1 evangelism is the evangelizing of people just like us. The only barrier to be crossed is the barrier of faith. This is the easiest type of evangelism because we already have a clear understanding of the people we are trying to win. Every Christian could be involved in this type of evangelism, and those with the gift of evangelist will be especially successful.

E-2 evangelism indicates that there are two barriers to be crossed. In addition to the barrier of faith is that of a different culture, similar yet different. These people are members of other homogeneous units, perhaps a different class or ethnic group, but we can still communicate with them in our language and share the gospel. Much of home mission work is in this category.

E-3 evangelism is related to people with an even greater cultural contrast, often with a language barrier as well. Reaching foreign university students is this kind of evangelism. Launching Korean churches in California is E-3 evangelism.

After this classification system had been used for a while, it became clear that there was another type of evangelism that had been totally left out. This is the evangelism of nominal members, people who are in the church but have never known the personal assurance of the salvation. It has been called *E-0 evangelism*. It calls our attention to the fact that there are millions of nominal

71

Christians who need to be won to Christ and that we should not take anyone's salvation for granted, not even in our own church. Peter Wagner refers to these as "functionally unchurched" persons.

Ethnic Ministries

A local church can get involved in ethnic ministry if it has some people who have the vision and gift for cross-cultural ministry. God gives people like this to the church. but we have to discover and train them. The whole church must be committed to making the adjustments that will come with the success of an ethnic ministry. It may mean broadening our style of worship and range of music. That might even be exciting! We should not expect ethnic converts to make unnecessary adjustments. In fact, we should strive for a pattern of *conversion with minimal cultural displacement,* so that they do not alienate themselves culturally from their unconverted ethnic friends but rather win them to Christ. Before long, we will discover that the new ethnic converts have enriched our lives and church and that the gospel works the same for them as it does for us—only for each of us within our own cultural framework.

In most communities, integrated churches are limited in their ability to evangelize minorities simply because most people prefer to find Christ among their own kind of people. However, an ethnic congregation can begin in an integrated congregation as a Sunday school class, then be launched as an ethnic church when many become true disciples.

One pattern that can be developed is a multi-congregational church like Los Angeles First Nazarene, in which an English-speaking congregation, a Spanish-speaking congregation, and a Korean congregation share the facilities of the same church building. In cities where land and building costs would be prohibitive for new ethnic congregations, such a plan may be the only viable way to do E-3 evangelism in an effective way. Some activities may be done together, such as baptism. But some other activities require too much cultural difference for satisfaction and are done separately, such as Communion, which the Hispanic Nazarenes do not like to hurry through.

White congregations can successfully evangelize Blacks and help get Black congregations going. "Anglo" churches can also develop a Spanish outreach by centering it in a Spanish Sunday school class or neighborhood Bible-study group. This is an important strategy for White/Anglo churches to consider prayerfully. An enormous percentage of the ethnic populations remain unevangelized. They have little opportunity to hear the gospel in their own cultural setting unless ethnic churches are multiplied through the vision and interest of White/Anglo churches.

Community Types and Church Types

How should churches apply the targeting principle to match the location, the congregation, and the community? We shall look at this issue by means of five church types, which are defined largely in terms of their community. The nature of the church's response to the community determines the future growth of the church.

1. *First Church*

First Church is identifiable by its philosophy of ministry. It considers the whole city or region its parish. It has a large but commuting membership including important people, excellent facilities centrally located, a well-known pastor, and fine staff. Yet it periodically has had problems of a declining attendance.

It used to be a family church, but a majority of its families now live in the suburbs. Problems of getting children and teens in to the church for activities have resulted in the loss of a good number of families to other churches. An increasing percentage of the children in the church are brought in from the neighborhood by Sunday school outreach programs, including a bus ministry, but few of their parents have been reached. The neighborhood now has many Black families or other ethnic minorities. It is becoming increasingly evident that First Church can only continue to exist in this location by continuous recruitment programs.

First Church faces the choice of relocating near where its family members live or of targeting on the available responsive people in the area with multiple-focus programs that are need-oriented. It needs to foster small-cell fellowship groups for increased intimacy. It may need to adapt its style of worship to that with which the community people can identify and respond.

2. New Church

New Church is a small but growing home mission church. There is a sense of excitement and intimacy in its services.

New Church needs to put a priority on developing a membership class. The people need to be helped to discover their spiritual gifts so the church will have the workers it needs. Every member is important.

There may be some E-0 evangelism to be done, with new people coming into the congregation from other churches. It must have both short-range and long-range building plans to keep up with its growth, or it may soon hit a ceiling of growth caused by "sociological strangulation."

3. Changing Church

This church is named for what is happening in its neighborhood. Actually, its problem is that the neighborhood has been changing but the church hasn't. But it will, one way or another. Its difference from First Church is primarily that it has never considered the whole city its parish but was originally a neighborhood church. It is an older church with second- and third-generation members who stick with the church out of loyalty or family ties. Its membership and attendance have been declining for several years so that its facilities are much larger than it needs. Only the building belongs to them—the neighborhood now belongs to another group with whom they have little effective contact. They are suffering from *ethnikitis*.

There are several alternatives: *(a)* relocation; *(b)* shift to a community-oriented ministry; or *(c)* disband the present congregation and build a new congregation from the new ethnic group. The second alternative would be very difficult for them, considering their history. Both of the last two alternatives would require a pastor with a gift for cross-cultural ministry, unless an ethnic pastor could be obtained. Actually, the situation might have some tremendous possibilities for people with a vision. Inner-city and ethnic churches that are built on church-growth strategy often have exciting growth. The issue is to develop a proper focus and sensitive targeting.

4. *Suburban Church*

Suburban Church is a New Church that succeeded in the suburbs. It is a growing church in a growing community where the families are. It is pretty much of a neighborhood church, though some people drive in from a distance just to be part of this congregation. Because of its continuing growth, it has a perennial problem of space shortage; but with a large acreage it keeps building to meet the need. Its finances are adequate for maintenance of the status quo, but often inadequate for expansion. It may eventually challenge First Church in membership.

75

It keeps a people flow coming into the church through special attractions, contacts of members in the community, and even through recommendation from community friends. The shepherd-type pastor and his staff are well known and active in the community. People like the church so well that there is danger of *koinonitis,* as Peter Wagner calls it, or overdeveloped fellowship, in which people so enjoy the "nice" people of their own congregation that they fail to go out and bring in the "new" people that God wants in His church. Emphasis should be laid on leading new converts into the life of holiness, training and deployment in evangelism, and a challenge to church planting.

5. *Rural Church*

The problem of church growth in the rural areas is too few people, too far apart, and too infrequent contact with each other because of the distances. Rural Church is probably one of three contrasting types.

a. Open Country Church once thrived as a center of community life before the exodus to the city began in earnest. It still flourishes in a few locations due to a dynamic pastor, a strong homogeneous unit tradition, or preference for its style by people who have moved to a nearby city or town. There is often a tenacious determination to keep the church going at all costs as a preserver and advocate of their way of life as a bulwark against the corruption of urban life. Homecoming Sunday is one of the greatest days of its year. This picture may be changing in many places, however, because of a return to the country.

b. Small Town Church may have problems and opportunities almost identical with those of Open Country Church. The only difference may be its location—in town instead of in open country—the bulk of its members driving into town for services and other activities. Or it may really be a town church and share characteristics with the neighborhood church in the city. If the population is declining, one of its principal problems may be competition with other churches. But it should be alert to discover any individuals or groups that are not being served or contacted by other churches.

c. Open Country Church or Small Town Church could become an *Ex-Rural Church* if the city engulfs it, or if the current city exodus invades the community. Resort areas may experience this invasion yearly during their tourist season. Suddenly people are available in the community where for decades an old, stable church had little possibility of growth. What will happen depends upon whether the congregation wants change or not. Oldtimers must learn to see newcomers as an opportunity for evangelism and growth. The church that makes them welcome and begins to minister to their spiritual needs is going to grow. Congregational life will have to become a fresh synthesis of old and new. The building-focus will have to become a people-focus. One of the most powerful unifying elements in the church can be the vision and involvement of both groups in winning the other newcomers to Christ and the church.

ACTION STEPS

1. *Something to Discuss*

a. Why is the concept of homogeneous units important for understanding church growth?

b. Why not just witness and win people to Christ? Why worry about targeting?

c. What are some of the advantages of E-1 and E-0 evangelism?

d. What are some of the special gifts that people need

to be successful in E-2 and E-3 evangelism and church planting?

e. Which of the five church types described fits your church the best? Discuss other characteristics of your church that make it unique.

f. How many constituents live more than 12 minutes away from the church? How many new converts joined the church last year who live within the 12-minute travel radius? How many from beyond the 12-minute radius?

2. *Something to Do*

a. Get one subcommittee going on a survey of the primary homogeneous units represented in your church, including the Sunday school.

b. Get another subcommittee to make a survey of the primary homogeneous units in your community. Then compare the two lists. Is your church a reasonable reflection of your community, or are some homogeneous units lacking? How can they be reached?

c. Is your church a broad-spectrum church or a narrow-spectrum church? If yours is a broad-spectrum church, what means do you have of focusing on the various groups within your church?

d. Take a vote in your groups as to which of the five church types your church most nearly resembles. If you think your church type is different from any of the five, give it a name and describe what you think is distinctive about it. List both similarities and differences between your church and the five types that are written up.

3. *Something to Read*

Engel, James F., and Norton, H. Wilbert. *What's Gone Wrong with the Harvest?* pp. 23-42, targeting.

Jones, Ezra Earl. *Strategies for New Churches,* pp. 34-57, church types.

McGavran, Donald A. *Understanding Church Growth,* pp. 183-215, culture and church growth.

McGavran, Donald, and Arn, Win. *How to Grow a Church,* pp. 111-67, church types.

Schaller, Lyle E. *Hey, That's Our Church!* pp. 51-90, church types.

5

Preparing for Sustained Growth

The church that keeps on growing has met at least four requirements for continuous growth: (1) It is meeting the needs of people in the community, or they would go elsewhere; (2) It has found a way to multiply its outreach; (3) It has developed in its organization as it has grown in size and moved to higher plateaus of growth possibilities; (4) It has remained dependent upon and obedient to the Holy Spirit. Let us see how these four requirements work out.

Meeting the Needs of People

1. *Balanced Ministries*

The larger church with sustained growth has a balance of ministries for all ages and interests that attract both families and singles. There is a place for everyone, and everyone can find an opportunity for ministry according to his gifts.

The small church, however, should not worry about having a well-rounded balance of programs. The small church can concentrate on meeting one need at a time. Meeting and filling needs will create demand for greater service.

2. *Specialties*

In addition to the comfortable feeling that one's needs are being satisfied, most growing churches have at least one *specialty* that stands out above all the rest. Most church members, and sometimes community people, can quickly identify it. It has often been the "sparking element" that triggered their surge of growth in the first place

---

FOUR ESSENTIALS
for Sustained Growth

1. Meet people's needs

2. Multiply units of outreach

3. Organize to grow

4. Depend upon and obey
    the Holy Spirit

---

and is a need that a responsive segment in the community recognizes and appreciates. Rapidly growing churches generally excel in several specialties.

Growth Through Multiplying Groups

When people become part of the church, they do so at a given time, in a given place, and join a given group of people with whom they feel at home. If we can multiply these groups, then the church can grow faster than if we had only one original group.

Peter Wagner has pointed out that a church needs different kinds and sizes of groups for different purposes. He has categorized these as celebration, congregation, and cell. *Celebration* gives us *church identity* in company with all the people of God in joyful public worship. *Congregation* gives us *group identity* as when we come together as Christians with people we know and who know us. We are at home with them. (This may be Sunday school class organization in large churches.) Small *cell groups* give us *personal identity* as we minister to each other at this intimate level.

In the very small church, all three functions may be fulfilled with the same group of people. But as the church grows, the increasing size of numbers makes the intimate relationship more difficult. Forming small congregations within the total fellowship of the church can meet that need and, incidentally, increase the potential for more growth. Sometimes Sunday school classes are small enough to fulfill cell functions, but often we need to form cell groups such as prayer cells and circles of concern.

In his excellent book *Let Your Church Grow,* Millard Reed points out that with the disappearance of the extended family of relatives in our day, there is still a hunger for "a sphere of intimacy" which the small group of the church is admirably fitted to fulfill. It is here that people

SPHERES OF INFLUENCE AND INTIMACY*

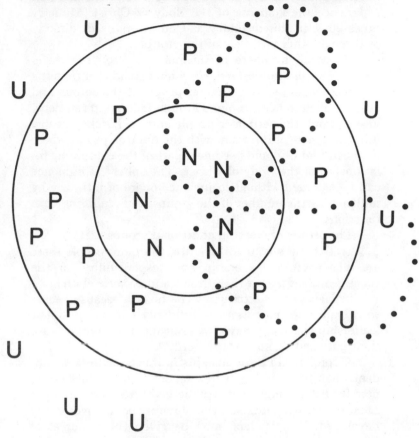

N = Nucleus (Committed core of church)
P = Perimeter (Those in occasional contact with the church.)
U = Unchurched

*From *Let Your Church Grow,* by Millard Reed. Beacon Hill Press of Kansas City, 1977.

develop satisfying social and spiritual relationships and experience the koinonia of the Body of Christ. Ministry takes place in this intimacy as God meets needs directly or through other members of the group.

But such a sphere of intimacy is also "the warm center of a *sphere of influence*" which extends out from the nucleus people to the perimeter people of the church and even to unchurched people. Through fellowship relations, love can pull the perimeter people and unchurched people into the sphere of intimacy with the nucleus people where they can find God and become a part of the continuing relationship of the Body of Christ. The sphere of influence can be enlarged without losing the sphere of intimacy by multiplying the number of the groups, thus fulfilling both functions.

The results of creating additional groups are:

1. The more groups there are, the more people there are who exercise leadership and responsibility for the success and growth of their group and of their church;

2. New groups often grow the fastest because people with leadership potential are suddenly released into new leadership space and have the exciting opportunity to use their gifts and talents for the Lord.

A corollary to these insights is that growth is dependent upon the training of new leadership. In most cases, new leadership must not just be given responsibility—it must be *trained.* Gifts and talents must be discovered and developed. New leaders must be given the resources of new concepts, skills, and methods to help them be successful in their areas of responsibility. Every growing church must have a constant program of both formal and informal training of new leaders. We learn best from models. Older members with responsibility can multiply their lay ministry by modeling the best in stewardship and leadership to younger members, preparing them for service.

84

There are many different kinds of groups in the church, but most of them fall into one of three classifications: (1) *Nurture groups,* like a prayer cell or neighborhood Bible study; (2) *Service groups,* like the choir, Sunday school classes, or ushers; and (3) *Outreach groups,*

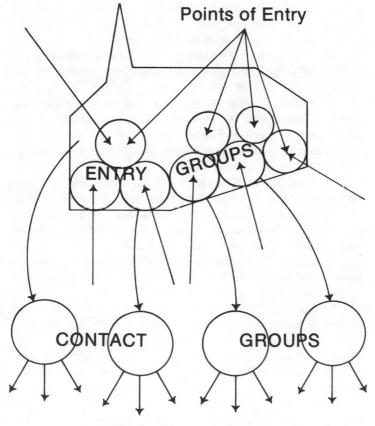

Points of Entry

ENTRY GROUPS

CONTACT GROUPS

Points of Contact

like extension classes in unreached neighborhoods. Some groups could fit into more than one classification.

There are two kinds of *outreach groups* that every church needs: (1) Those that can serve as *points of contact* for evangelism; (2) Those that can serve as *points of entry* for getting new people into the church. Some can serve *both purposes.* Many of these *contact points* and *entry points* are used by many in the church's program. When we see their function clearly, these groups can help us accelerate our church growth even more.

Dr. Raymond Hurn shares with us the following examples of points of contact for sustained growth in the church.

1. A large number of churches, and especially pastors, carry on counseling and other ministries to various groups of people that have problems or are lonely. This results in counseling on marriage problems, adult singles, divorcees, broken homes, runaway teenagers, etc.

2. Specific activities have involved bringing in a professional psychologist to lecture on how to communicate; running busses to baseball games; taking teenagers roller-skating; and in other ways, helping persons so they can have a point of contact with the church.

3. Especially in the smaller communities, the church pastor or church member can have considerable influence in the community in points of contact.

In one small Washington community, the local doctor introduced the pastor to the Chamber of Commerce in a meeting. The pastor realized that these businessmen met there every week and so he continued to go to the Chamber of Commerce meetings. Eventually, they elected him secretary, then treasurer, then vice-president, and finally president. This gave him a point of contact with the stable decision-making part of the community—the businessmen. The pastor later joined the Toastmasters Club and the Kiwanis Club—all of this in a effort to keep in touch with the men of the community. They liked him; he often stopped and had coffee with them. Although they sometimes smoked their cigars and rolled their dice in his presence, when trouble came in their marriages or a child ran away from home, they did not hesitate to call out to the pastor of that church for guidance and help.

4. Community- or state-operated schools for physically handicapped and mentally retarded are points of contact for a caring, loving ministry to entire families.

5. The Alcoholics Anonymous organization has been the point of contact that has led some of our churches into a redemptive ministry in their community.

Like other organizations mentioned in this section, "AA" relates to communities of 2,000 to 10,000 population, as well as to larger metro areas. The small towns (and that's where 75 percent of our churches are located) have needs just like the cities, and points of contact can be made.

In the larger cities, involvement in community affairs does not seem to rate nearly as high with most of our people. In small cities, wholesome community-wide activities form points of contact that cause people in the community to think well of the church and its people.

6. We still have many lay-type ministers in small towns where good business practices and honesty and fair dealing in business have formed points of contact for the church.

7. Being available when tragedy strikes is an important ministry for Christians. In one Ozark community, the church intentionally set about to help people at a time of tragedy. A brooder house on a small chicken ranch burned. The pastor and the church men got community men together and they had an old-fashioned "barn raising" type of activity, and they rebuilt the brooder house.

Later, a farmer's barn burned. Again, the church came in to organize people to clean up the mess and rebuild the barn.

One day an elderly lady's home burned to the ground. She barely made it out alive, losing her dentures and eyeglasses in the process. Neighbors took her in for the night and the neighbors called the pastor of the Church of the Nazarene who went over immediately and gave her $25.00. Later, the whole church discussed her plight and decided they wanted to do something to help her and so they voted to replace her dentures (a cost of $300). When the announcement was made from the pulpit, the money all came in in one day. It made not only a contact with a grateful elderly lady and all of her friends and relatives, but it also made an impression on a dentist.

The small community had no ambulance. A tragedy occurred and a Nazarene loaned a station wagon to take a person to the hospital 60 miles away. The church took over the organization of a campaign to buy an ambulance for the community.

8. Laymen are often involved in vocations that could form points of contact. They are teachers, firemen, vocational school teachers or administrators, sports directors, etc. There is a web of communication, even in large cities, among these groups. In New York City, the policemen have a newspaper of their own. One church (not Nazarene) discovered this and began to communicate with the policemen through their own news media and announced a day to honor policemen. Thirty or 40 policemen and their families came out to church that day, and a number of families have since been brought into the fellowship of the church.

In Salem, Ore., First Church, Rev. Holland London gives great attention to the specialized needs of small groups. He spends a great deal of time with men, especially in early morning breakfast and prayer sessions, as well as in luncheon meetings. He gives attention not only to the business community, but to the clerical, blue-collar worker, and professional group as well.

In larger churches, there is greater opportunity for establishment of various contact groups. Some of these, however, can be done in small churches. Here are a few more contact groups that have proved helpful in Nazarene churches:

 a. Mothers' clubs for expectant mothers or new mothers
 b. Children's Bible clubs
 c. Young mothers' Bible clubs
 d. Tape ministry to shut-ins
 e. A special outreach to racial minorities through Bible study contacts or Sunday school class
 f. Halfway houses ministering to alcoholics, drug addicts, and others
 g. Family gym night, either at a local school or in the church gym
 h. Thrift shop, especially useful in depressed areas where clothing may be made available at little or no cost
 i. Participation in parades with floats, displays, etc.
 j. Bible studies for adult singles
 k. Golden Agers' clubs
 l. Fellowship through sports
 m. Helping newcomers to the community find housing and jobs
 n. Day-care and nursery centers
 o. Ministry in nursing homes to the elderly

Entry groups that are already part of the internal functions of the church are important points of entry into the church for the incorporation of new converts or for getting unconverted contacts into the church fellowship for internal evangelism. New people can enter these groups and become part of them immediately. However, this function of entry doesn't happen automatically—the new people must be made to feel part of the group through individual and group acceptance and opportunity to participate. They must feel that they are wanted and needed. Here are some of these groups:

1. New convert classes (in the Sunday school or during the week)
2. Christian Life Division groups (Sunday school classes, youth groups, Caravan, etc.) and missionary groups
3. Bible study and/or prayer groups for nurture
4. Support groups (secretaries, etc.)
5. Ushers

Additional. groups that can serve *both as internal points of entry and points of contact* are:

6. The choir and other musical groups (including outreach programs)
7. Ladies' groups (like "Buttons and Bows" serving feminine interests)
8. Men's fellowships (for fellowship, evangelism, and missions interest)
9. Deaf ministry (reaching also their families)
10. Special education ministry (services, using teens to tutor)
11. Day-care ministry (reaching back to the parents)
12. Christian school ministry (reaching the whole family)

New converts can enter into these ministries and find a place of service as well as opportunity for participation in evangelism.

For help in getting circles of concern or an evangelistic Bible study program started, see the books recommended at the end of this chapter.

The Growth Cycle

Churches that keep on growing must break through from one growth plateau to another, or they will level off at the size their organizational structure can support.

1. *The Five Growth Levels*

The membership figures for these levels are only approximate and vary considerably from one church to another, but the organizational structure is where the real contrasts are between the stages.

a. *The small church* (up to 74 members—57.3 percent of Nazarene churches) is not unique to the Church of the Nazarene. All denominations have a majority of small churches. Fifty percent of all the 330,000 churches in America have fewer than 75 in attendance on Sunday. They can be static or dynamic. Many of them are relatively new churches and will soon be medium-sized churches. Members are typically strongly committed to Christ and the church as evidenced by their faithful attendance, sacrificial giving, and loyal service as workers in the church's programs. The quality of the fellowship is what appeals to many people. In its sphere of intimacy everyone is known and everyone is important.

There are two requirements for a congregation to jump the barrier between being a small church and a medium church: (1) It must grow rapidly enough in members and finance that it can support a full-time pastor; (2) It must be willing to move from being one large group to being a number of smaller groups where intimacy can more easily be developed.

b. *The medium church* (75-199 members—32.8 percent of Nazarene churches) has a *full-time pastor* and is composed of several congregations. It has learned how to absorb new people and it is building a balanced ministry to

91

FIVE STAGES OF GROWTH LEVELS

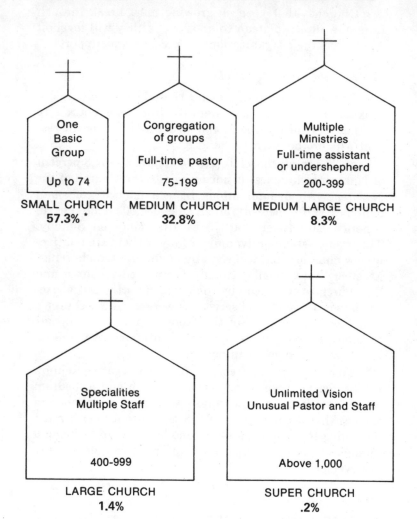

One
Basic
Group

Up to 74

SMALL CHURCH
57.3% *

Congregation
of groups

Full-time pastor

75-199

MEDIUM CHURCH
32.8%

Multiple
Ministries

Full-time assistant
or undershepherd

200-399

MEDIUM LARGE CHURCH
8.3%

Specialities
Multiple Staff

400-999

LARGE CHURCH
1.4%

Unlimited Vision
Unusual Pastor and Staff

Above 1,000

SUPER CHURCH
.2%

*Percentage of Nazarene churches of this size in 1976.

all ages. Often a new set of more capable leaders gradually takes over. It has probably gotten involved in a building program and is carrying a heavy financial debt. The upper membership limits of this stage are about as big as a church can become with one pastor and his lay leaders. In order to move from being a medium church to being a medium-large church, it must grow rapidly enough in membership and finance to need and want a full-time assistant or develop a well-organized lay shepherding program to help in the pastoral (caring) ministry.

c. *The medium-large church* (200-399—8.3 percent of Nazarene churches) may be too big for one full-time pastor to handle unless excellent use of lay workers is utilized, so it may start this stage of growth with its first *full-time associate,* sometimes drawn from its own ranks of achieving lay persons. The choice of the first full-time associate is a crucial one for the continued growth of the church. Without him or her the church cannot easily continue to grow. Of course, the associate must be capable of contributing directly or indirectly to the continued growth of the church. The first associate should be not just a performer and organizer, but especially a trainer and enabler who can multiply the outreach and maintenance ministries of the church through its laymen. The medium-large church must cope with its growth by developing and maintaining a full program of balanced ministries to attract and retain new people.

In order to move on to the large-church stage, it must do two things. It must develop adequate go-structures for recruitment and evangelism, and it must grow sufficiently to need and afford a multiple staff.

d. *The large church* (400-999—1.4 percent of Nazarene churches) is characterized by a *catalytic pastor* and a *multiple staff* who guide the development and function of the *specialities* of a *broad-spectrum ministry with a multi-*

ple focus. If shepherding groups (circles of concern) have not been developed at earlier states, it is crucial to further growth that they be developed to meet the needs for care, intimacy, and personal identity that only a small group relationship can provide. A satellite structure of external groups for nurture and evangelism becomes increasingly necessary. Some of these satellites may develop the potential for becoming daughter churches eventually. Meanwhile they will contribute to the expansion growth of the church.

e. The super church (above 1,000—.2 percent of Nazarene churches) seems to differ from the large church in the following ways. It has an *extraordinarily gifted pastor* to whom leaders and people are tremendously loyal. It has capitalized on the right timing in local identity and the meeting of felt community needs. It has adequate facilities in a prominent location. It has an *unlimited vision* for growth and a ministry to the total community, to its denomination, and to the world. Super churches have the potential for becoming great church-planting congregations responsible for the parenting of dozens of additional churches in their areas.

2. *Location and Capacity*

In considering location, there are three things to keep in mind. *Visibility* is worth the money it costs—it tells people you exist and where you are located. Church property should be *accessible* from two directions, if possible, for ease of entry and exit. The intersection of two main streets or roads is excellent. Your needs for *room to grow* depend on your vision and goals, but they set limits for your ultimate growth.

Capacity is related to the size of the church property and the building restrictions placed on it, the usable space of the buildings, and the size of the parking lot. The rule of thumb for space is that when attendance reaches 80 percent of capacity, it will limit growth. When that point is reached, what can be done? You may *increase space* by a building program, by more efficient use of available space, or by scattering—especially for Sunday school—to use other nearby facilities. Or it may be time to start a branch Sunday school or church. *Increased use* of your facilities may be worked out through multiple sessions or staggered sessions.

3. *Personal and Congregational Goals*

Should every church grow to the point of being a super church? Or even a large church? The analogy of Body Life is a help to us here. Every church has its own potential and should have its own history without comparison with other churches as long as it is growing and functioning according to its possibilities. Every large metro area needs a super church, some large churches, medium churches, and many small churches. They help each other. The high visibility and reputation of the super church helps the identity of the small church, but the small church is doing a job of nurture and evangelism that the super church cannot do.

Some of us are more at home in a small or medium church, but this does not have to stifle growth. There is always the exciting potential of helping to parent a new congregation and thus contribute to the growth of the Kingdom. Growing churches plant growing churches— like parent, like child. Some of us as individuals may make a career—as pastors or laymen—of helping to start new home mission churches, or helping to get a static church off dead center and growing again. And some may feel called to start with a new congregation, grow with it as it grows, make the adjustments of each new stage of growth, and see that church grow into a dynamic holiness church with a ministry that is felt around the world. Let's let God choose how He wants to use us, but give it all we have.

The Church-Growth Leader

A Spirit-filled pastor is the key to local church growth. He must want the church to grow and be willing to pay the price for it. His people must also be willing to pay the price for growth. The pastor intends that the church shall grow because he is concerned about the lost of his community. He believes that God wants his church to grow.

The 1977 surveys by Dr. Raymond Hurn identified factors accounting for growth in the ministry and evangelism in the "growingest" Nazarene churches. The top four characteristics included: (1) A shepherd-type pastoral ministry; (2) A pastor who had good personal relationships in the church and community; (3) A pastor who was supported by a church membership that also had good personal relations among themselves and in their community; and (4) A pastor and members who were effective in developing need-centered outreach ministries.

Characteristics of the pastoral leadership reinforced the factors by describing the pastor himself as one who (1) Could delegate responsibility and authority to many persons in the church; (2) Encouraged "feedback" from his people; (3) Was seen as a strong leader; and (4) Developed shepherd-type ministries among paid staff and/or volunteer workers.

Pastors in growing churches are not always seen as "great preachers," though they are always good communicators, thus keeping open the lines of communication to and from the people in the pew.

Length of Pastorate

In the churches with the 10 largest Sunday schools in America, Elmer Towns discovered a few years ago that the average length of pastorate was 22 years and one month. Being large and growing are two different things, but in this case all of these churches had tremendous growth. Many of them had had no other pastor than their present pastor.

When a church is growing, one of the biggest threats to that growth is a change of pastors. One of the common characteristics of small churches that have existed for a number of years and are still small is the frequency with which there have been pastoral changes. The short pastorate (less than five years) is a serious deterrent to the development of sustained growth in a local church. Lyle Schaller says that the fifth, sixth, seventh, and eighth years are the most productive years of the typical pastorate.

Dr. Raymond Hurn reports that in research with pastors of our growingest churches in every area of North America, he has been impressed over and over again with the length of term of pastors in these churches—5 to 12 years is the usual range for churches with strong growth.

Twenty-two years is probably an unusually long pastorate for most pastors and most churches, but 5 to 12 years seems more workable. A church needs the continuity of a longer-than-average pastorate to help it move out of one stage of growth and into another. Obviously no one but the Lord knows what the ideal length of pastorate would be for a given congregation and a given pastor. But many churches have failed to realize their potential in growth because of pastorates that were too short.

Within the Lord's guidance, how can a local church and a pastor help to lengthen the pastorate so that there can be a greater probability of continued growth? To begin with, both pastor and people should make not only short-range growth plans but also long-range growth plans to keep both parties challenged and excited about the potential of the future.

The pastor could grasp opportunity for personal and professional growth through continuing education in specialized seminars or short courses from his college or seminary. A sabbatical as long as six months or a year may be impractical for both church and pastor, but a breakaway of a couple of months every few years might save a pastor to a church that loves him and wants him to stay on and be their church-growth leader. The pastor himself might carefully reflect, the next time a call comes from another church, that his greatest opportunity for being used of the Lord to build a great, growing church might lie right where he is.

Spiritual Factors in Church Growth

1. *Revival and Church Growth*

There are times when a wise pastor and people in a growing church know that revival is necessary. They must expect it, pray for it, believe for it—and obey. There must be a mighty moving of God's Spirit to push the church on to a new level of spiritual life. This expectancy—this insistence—on periodic revival must become part of the rhythm of spiritual life in the growing church. Only God's Spirit can keep bringing the renewal that is necessary to maintaining a growth pattern in any church.

God can do in a moment in revival what we have not been able to do for years. God often sends revival when there is a new emphasis on His Word, prayer, openness, and the ministry of the Holy Spirit. We cannot program revival any more than we can program growth. However, we can prepare for it and not be surprised when it comes. We must pray to God for revival and not be satisfied until it comes.

2. *When Revival Comes*

a. Harness it for permanent and continuing results. Help it spread to other groups and to other places.

b. Train new converts for the role of witness to maximize their evangelism potential to their unconverted friends.

c. Get Christians organized to follow up those who have experienced spiritual victories.

d. Urge those who have been saved to go on to holiness.

e. Move immediately into action to get new converts incorporated into the church as responsible members.

f. Be ready for church planting when new opportunities open up among groups who have responded to God's Spirit.

When revival comes, it is often "the sparking element" that results in great church growth that can be sustained, spread, and intensified in results over a period of years. "O Lord, revive thy work in the midst of the years, in the midst of the years make known; in wrath remember mercy" (Hab. 3:2).

ACTION STEPS

1. *Something to Discuss*

a. What would you say is the "specialty" that stands out as the distinctive program or ministry of your church?

b. How are the needs of celebration, congregation, and cell met in your church?

c. How does the "sphere of intimacy" build the church?

d. What are the contact groups and entry groups that are working in your church?

e. What are the factors that set limits to the size of a congregation?

f. What should a growing church be like in its atmosphere and spiritual life?

g. How does revival fit into church-growth strategy?

2. *Something to Do*

a. List one contact group and one entry group that you do not have in your church at present which you think would have good potential for your community and church. Do some "imagineering" in developing a proposal as to how they might be started.

b. Locate your church in the five stages of growth levels. Decide where you want your church to be in 5 years, in 10 years. Chart the necessary organizational steps that must be taken to get you there.

c. List the factors that might limit the size of your church membership in the near present or future. Decide what can be done about these.

3. *Something to Read*

McGavran, Donald A. *Understanding Church Growth,* pp. 163-80, on revival and church growth, including the cross-cultural setting.

Reed, Millard. *Let Your Church Grow:* A Brief Study of Church Growth Principles as Related to "Circles of Concern," 40 pages. Excellent.

Shanafelt, Ira L. *The Evangelical Home Bible Class.* A manual for leaders.

Wagner, C. Peter. *Your Church Can Grow,* pp. 84-96, growth size; pp. 97-109, celebration, congregation, and cell.

6

Planting Churches For New Growth

Today we have vastly expanded our potential for carrying out the Great Commission. We have not, however, been able to improve upon the basic strategy of church planting which propelled Christianity from a group of 12 believers to a world-changing church in only a few years.

The first wave of church planting was probably more spontaneous than planned, as far as the people involved were concerned. Certainly the mind of God had conceived the plan, for the 3,000 believers who accepted Christ as their Messiah and Lord at Pentecost were soon to carry the message back to all parts of the Mediterranean world.

The next wave of church planting happened when persecution scattered the believers throughout Judea and Samaria, except for the apostles who remained in Jerusalem (Acts 8:1).

Then God instituted another pattern by choosing individuals for the deliberate, intentional planting of churches. He sent Philip to Samaria. He started Paul and Barnabas and many others on church-planting trips across the known world. Many of these church planters' names are not known to us today. But somehow they got churches started in all the major cities of their time during that first generation of Christians, and their churches have multiplied and spread.

The Church of the Nazarene owes its record of rapid growth more to rapid church planting than to any other factor. In 1907, there were 99 churches and 6,198 members. In 1908, at the end of a consolidation year and launching of the denomination, there were 288 churches and 10,414 members. Then in rapid order we multiplied churches. The 288 churches doubled in four years to 576, and doubled again nine years later when 1,145 were reported. By 1936, the number of churches had again doubled.

By 1959, the denomination had 4,696 churches and membership totaled 311,299. This did not account for the excellent work being done on world mission fields, where by 1972 we had 1,377 churches, and a total of 6,333 worldwide. World membership totaled 605,185 in 1976, and churches numbered 6,736 worldwide. But the pace of growth in Great Britain, Canada, and the United States was slowing down.

In 1973, in his book *Mission Possible,* Dr. Raymond W. Hurn warned of a downturn in Nazarene growth "as a result of disorganizations without compensating new organizations." Denominational survival demands that we plant new churches at a rate of at least 50 per year, for that's about how fast we close dying churches.

In the 12 years from 1960 to 1972, 720 new churches were organized; however, there was a net gain of only 95. Our denomination has leveled off in its growth in the U.S.A. Can we turn the charts upward again? Our greatest growth occurred while we were concentrating on reaching poor people and while launching hundreds of churches.

102

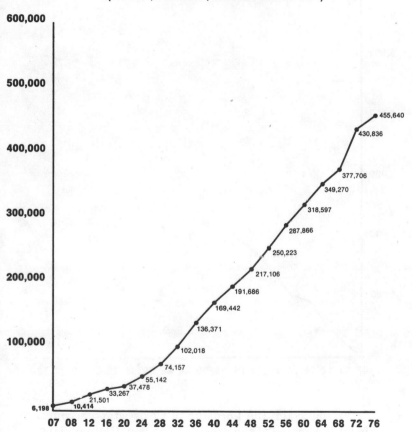

Membership Growth
Church of the Nazarene
1907-1976
(U.S.A., Canada, and Great Britain)

600,000

500,000

455,640
430,836
400,000
377,706
349,270
318,597
300,000
287,866
250,223
217,106
200,000
191,686
169,442
136,371
100,000
102,018
74,157
55,142
37,478
33,267
21,501
6,198
10,414

07 08 12 16 20 24 28 32 36 40 44 48 52 56 60 64 68 72 76

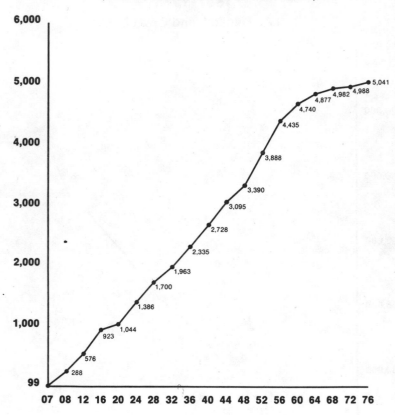

Growth in Number of Churches
Church of the Nazarene
1907-1976

(U.S.A., Canada, and Great Britain)

We who claim the Lordship of Christ stand accountable for the spread of the gospel in our day. Church planting is the means by which people in increasing numbers

104

can find Jesus in places where before there was no one to tell them of the Savior's love. Involvement in church planting is not just the responsibility of church officials or even pastors; it is the joy and privilege of every member of the Body of Christ. It was intended to be part of your ministry and mine.

We are in an excellent position to really get growing and maximize the potential that we have for reaching others. As we plant more churches, the result will be a dramatic increase in our overall growth rate.

The New York and Virginia districts planted more churches from 1972 to 1976 than any others. These same two districts are at the top of the decadal growth charts in composite membership for the denomination. Leaders in church planting are found time and again among the leaders in membership growth.

Growing districts plant churches. New churches make growing districts.

One of our highest priorities must be to discover how churches are being successfully planted today, and to go out and do it ourselves. The exciting part of this new day of church planting is that every Nazarene can personally get involved in helping to plant a new church in the near future.

Sometimes it is the district that initiates the plans for a new church. At other times, the new church will spring out of opportunities that are recognized and developed within a local church. Sometimes the opportunity for a new church will be realized when a Nazarene family moves into a new community and discovers no holiness church there.

Always the pastor and district superintendent are involved. The excitement generated by the new church is often enough to bring new life to an entire district. Volunteer teams from across the district pitch in to help. Spiritual benefits are reaped across the district.

But principally, the new church itself enjoys the special spirit of divine joy that comes from being workers together with God in creating a new outpost for His ministry among men.

Sometimes the formative days of a new church are under the supervision of district officers and boards. At other times it is under the immediate supervision of the pastor and board of a local church until the daughter congregation is ready to be organized as a local church. "Organizing" a local church is the responsibility of the district superintendent.

Four Basic Questions

Whoever is laying the plans for a new church will need to seek answers to four basic questions before the "planting" can really begin.

1. Are there communities of people similar in nature to those attending the existing church but beyond at least a 15-minute travel time? As previously noted, the most effective range for a local church is within 12 minutes' travel time. Such outlying communities provide prime targets for church planting.

2. Are there communities of people who have different cultural or ethnic backgrounds from the existing congregation and who are not now being effectively reached? Such communities provide opportunities for bridging growth.

3. Are there classes of people within your present community who are not being reached because they are from a different economic or subcultural grouping from the majority of your congregation? What do these people think of your Christian witness? Could you start outreach classes or congregations among these people?

106

4. Have you studied and discussed in depth the Great Commission in connection with the purpose of your church in its community?

Questions such as these are basic to church planting. After they have been thoroughly resolved, it is time to go into procedural matters, or methodology. Then such questions as the following must be asked and answered:

- Who will plant the new church?
- Where will it be planted?
- When should it be planted?
- How should it be planted and how much will it cost?

A growing body of expertise in church planting exists in the Church of the Nazarene. Most of our district superintendents are qualified by experience and by graduate-level training to act as consultants in church growth for their districts. More and more of our pastors have received similar training. Thousands of laymen will soon be trained in the basic principles of church growth through the Christian Service Training program.

We know how Nazarene churches have been born and how they have grown successfully and given birth to other new churches. We are able to diagnose why churches grow and why they die.

Here are some models of church planting that have proven success records in Nazarene churches.

Church Planting Through a Local Church

Some prospering churches have set and kept a goal of starting one new congregation each year. Some churches add a new assistant pastor to their staff periodically in order to train him in their growth philosophy during the year and help him and some of their people to start a new congregation at the end of the year. Pastor Everett Baker at Roseburg, Ore., First Church has recently employed this method successfully. Thousands of new congregations can be started through local churches before the year 2000.

Parenting a church is the most common and natural way that local churches can start a new congregation. They see an opportunity for a new church in an adjacent neighborhood where they have a number of members. The members take up the challenge and start an outreach group in their neighborhood. The best talent in music, personal evangelism, youth work, and ministry are provided. The parent church helps raise whatever finances are necessary to rent facilities or purchase property. In two to five years, the new group has become self-supporting and the church is organized as a separate congregation about the time they are able to assume full self-support. The people have been trained in a growing congregation, and they make their church grow. A genuine holiness church is produced.

Olathe College Church of the Nazarene is an example of a fast-growing parent church which successfully started a new church in Olathe's Westside. Eleven years in advance of organizing the new church, the Olathe people faced a dynamic challenge of relocation and ministry to a new college community. Simultaneously, they committed themselves to launching a new church to help evangelize their growing suburban city. They bought a large tract of land on the west side (for the new church) while relocating their parent church on the east side of Olathe. The vision was one of multiplying the outreach.

The new church is healthy and growing and making plans for its own first buildings. After one year, the new church was reporting 106 members and the parent church had taken in approximately twice as many new members as they gave to start the new church.

The satellite model is a version of the parenting model that is probably the most widespread plan used today by

SATELLITE MODEL OF CHURCH PLANNING

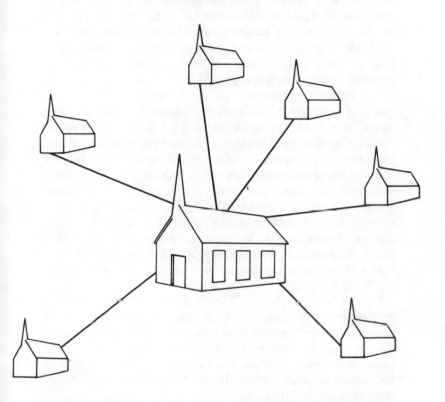

growing churches and movements around the world. Its value lies in the fact that it combines in its method the growth of the parent church by expansion and the potential for planting a new church as a result of this success. It is a model in which the local church gains a good part of its expansion growth through the multiplication of outreach groups in the neighborhoods of its members (such as "Circles of Concern" and evangelistic Bible study groups). When these groups grow, the local church grows—but also the outreach groups at a distance may become house churches with the future potential of full church organization. The satellite model multiplies the opportunity for lay leadership development. Some may sense a call to full-time ministry and continue on as the pastors of the new churches when they are organized.

The multi-congregational model works well in cities. Los Angeles First Church of the Nazarene offers a prime example of a church growing through the multi-congregational model. Four separate ethnic congregations share the same building on Sunday. In addition to the White/Anglo congregation, one Spanish-speaking and two Korean congregations share the same facilities. A Filipino congregation is being formed. The White/Anglo congregation usually has 30 nationalities represented in the 11 a.m. service. These prefer the integrated group to the segregated. In addition, outreach groups that minister to several groups, such as singles, are meeting at community locations away from the church.

New Milford, N.J., Church of the Nazarene demonstrates another application of the multi-congregational model. As it outgrew its facilities, outreach Sunday school classes were started in homes of members. Later, some eventually developed into new churches. The parent and its daughter churches combined have grown from 32 to 494 members in 10 years.

Brothering a church is a term invented by Dr. Raymond Hurn, executive director of the Department of Home Missions, to describe the possibilities of several nearby churches going in together to get a new church planted. In some cases, charter members are given by each of several churches and are fused into the nucleus for the new congregation. If enough members are given, it can start out as a self-supporting church from the beginning.

When a congregation moves to a new church facility at a new location, that congregation together with other nearby churches may help get a new congregation started in its old church building. This model is especially suited for starting ethnic churches in a changing neighborhood.

Virtually every district has some "Big Brother" models. Some larger churches have the capacity for helping a little brother all on their own. Pasadena, Calif., First Church is a good example of a church whose generosity to "Little Brother" has extended far beyond its own community to the east coast.

The colonization model will work for either district-initiated church planting or local church extension. It involves the decision of Christians to deliberately change the place of their residence so as to participate in the planting of a new church. It might mean buying a house in the suburb where the new congregation is to be planted. It might mean taking a job or getting a transfer to the community where a new church is starting. A retired railroad engineer with his wife moved to Horseshoe Bend, Ark., and began Bible studies in their mobile home. A growing new church resulted.

Some pastors and superintendents recruit college graduates just before commencement to get them to settle in their community to help in new or struggling churches.

The multiplication of highrise apartments and condominiums with their locked front doors and "No Solicitors" signs has presented a formidable barrier to urban evangelism. Many urban congregations have discovered, however, that this barrier can be surmounted by encouraging their people to move into different apartment complexes and condominiums where the church would like to evangelize or even start a new daughter congregation. The whole building or complex becomes their mission field, perhaps shared with another family or two who have moved there to join in the ministry. This approach has been used effectively by Nazarenes in New York City; Chicago; Washington, D.C.; and a variety of urban locations. Bible-study groups are started in each building. Later, when the group grows, perhaps a whole apartment is rented as a meeting place. Eventually, as the groups are moving toward organization as a congregation, the new pastor gets an apartment in another building to increase the potential of the outreach. Land and building in the downtown area may be prohibitive, but business property (office or store space, often on the ground floor of the apartment buildings) may be leased and remodeled for their purposes, and the new congregation is in business and conveniently located.

The district team model has been successful in planting hundreds of new churches. It typically involves the following components: (1) Appointment of workers by the district superintendent, (2) Establishment of a district Home Missions budget, and (3) Rapid construction of facilities, often before there is a congregation. Money is raised for subsidizing the beginning of the church through home mission budgets or a home mission fund-raising tour, and a budget is set for the needs of the new church. A location is chosen and facilities are found in which the new congregation can meet. A time schedule is set up with the anticipation of growth and development toward self-support. Usually district home mission funds are used to build a chapel as the initial unit, occasionally combining it with living quarters for the pastor and his family. The variations are many.

The nucleus to form the basis for the new congregation sometimes comes from a "swarm" of people from another Nazarene church in the area. Sometimes the "home mis-

112

sion pastor" from missionary motivation digs out a congregation himself. Often an evangelist is secured for a protracted meeting of several weeks with the intention of forming the new congregation from the converts.

Catalytic models involve people who help to get a church started but do not necessarily remain to become a part of the church as pastor or members. The "home mission pastor" who helps get the church started may also remain as its permanent pastor.

The catalytic church planter is someone who is experienced in going into a new neighborhood with few or no contacts and quickly gathering a nucleus of people together to form the beginning of a church. He is a person that people are attracted to and easily have confidence in. He combines the qualities of a pastor and evangelist, and is especially adept at personal evangelism.

Rev. Warren Rogers is using this approach to start new Nazarene churches in Black communities. He usually combines the personal contact approach with an evangelistic campaign, and has successfully started many churches. Other evangelists give a certain number of weeks each year for campaigns to help start new home mission churches in this catalytic pattern.

The most common type of Nazarene catalytic church planter is typically a pastor who has discovered that he has the cluster of gifts and skills to specialize in starting new churches. He stays with the fledgling congregation longer than just to gather it. He remains until it is stabilized and established in the community—the time varying from a number of months to a year or two. If he feels the Lord's leading, he may stay in one pastorate even longer. But the ministry that he is eager to get back to is starting a new church. Some of these pastors start many such churches in their lifetime of ministry. A number of successful pastors have elected to become new-church planters.

The fusion model is a method of church planting which many catalytic church planters use to get a congregation going. It consists of going into the selected neighborhood, starting a half dozen or more home Bible-study cells, then "fusing" them together into a congregation after a few weeks when the time has arrived to start regular church services. The approach is to go from door to door asking people if they would be interested in joining a home Bible-study group, or if they know of someone who might be interested. If the answer is affirmative, the next question is if they would be willing for one to be held in their home. In responsive neighborhoods, there is a high percentage of positive response. This approach can also be used for developing evangelistic Bible-study groups for the growth of an already established local church.

The Bible-study groups are formed independently of each other in various sections of the neighborhood and are informed about each other's existence without hiding the fact that the goal is eventually to establish a new church in the area. If there are Nazarenes in the community who can open their homes for the Bible-study groups, so much the better. But experience has shown that many non-Nazarenes are glad to cooperate in such a program and are even eager to help us get a church started, though they may remain affiliated with their own denomination. The Bible-study groups are a way to start, and they sometimes become part of the permanent outreach of the new congregation. This is the way Nazarene missionaries started the first church in Ecuador in the city of Guayaquil.

The task force model of church planting is characterized by a group of church members who deliberately decide to become a temporary task force for helping a new congregation get established and start to grow. The

114

parenting church loans some of its members for a period of time to provide the new congregation with instant membership (and hence, visibility), instant leaders, instant finances, and instant tradition (mature Nazarenes to serve as models for new Nazarenes). Some of the "loaned" members may stay on permanently, but usually would return to the home church in a year.

Some kinds of helpers are going to be there for only a limited term, as students in a summer ministries program; and college, Bible school, or seminary students who work in a local church until their studies are completed. There are dangers in the task force group keeping too much to themselves and being seen as "foreigners" by the local people. However, an emphasis on developing local leadership and getting the loan group to identify with the people can overcome the problems. The advantages are so great that such an opportunity should never be ignored.

Church-planting congregations can deliberately loan some of their gifted members to speed up the development and establishment of new churches. The rewards for these participating members might make it the finest experience of their lives. Some people who would not be prepared to join the new congregation permanently would be willing to serve for a specified time.

By whatever model a new church finds its way into existence, it faces many a challenge on its way to being a responsible, reproducing church. When asked by the district or local leaders, the department of Home Missions stands ready to provide counsel and direction for the new church.

The Department of Home Missions provides a number of services for mission congregations. Among these are: (1) A gift packet upon organization; (2) Letters of greeting and congratulation from the general superintendents and the Department; (3) Assistance with matters of incorpora-

115

tion; (4) Building helps for those planning a new building; (5) A General Church Loan for those new churches unable to secure commercial financing, and (6) Financial assistance to new churches holding their first vacation Bible school.

Churches which achieve significant growth records are recognized at district assemblies through the Growing Church Achievement Program sponsored by the department.

Home Missions *Alert* is a periodical devoted to church growth and contains much helpful data not found anywhere else. All of these helps and more are devised with but one goal in mind—that given to us by Jesus when He said "Go . . . make disciples."

The Supreme Task

Making disciples, the ultimate goal of evangelism and home missions, remains the supreme task of the Church. The promise, "Lo, I am with you alway," is for those who "Go . . . make disciples." Both the command and the promise are ours. Church planting is God's chosen way for us to multiply our efforts to win the lost of our generation. It is possible because Christ said, "I will build my church" (Matt. 16:18).

Church planting is an apostolic ministry. The apostles belonged to the whole Church and were concerned with its growth and expansion to the ends of the earth. We enter into their apostolic ministry when we no longer confine ourselves just to the interests of our local church, but lay a foundation for others in helping to plant new churches (1 Cor. 3:10-11).

John Wesley was such an apostle. He indicated this when he said, "The world is my parish." He understood church-growth principles—growth through the multiplication of small groups, lay ministry, winning the winnable. And he planted churches (societies, they were called) the length and breadth of Britain, and thereby changed the course of its history. His movement jumped the Atlantic and sent circuit riders racing out to the frontiers to get churches planted on the very edges of civilization.

In this generation, the Wesleyan mantle has fallen on us. If the world is again to see a great revival of the Wesleyan truths of holiness, perfect love, and the sanctifying fulness of the Holy Spirit, we are the ones who will have to pay the price to be used of God to spread it. The power of such a movement can come only from a mighty surge of church growth and church planting empowered by God's Spirit. We can literally see God change the course of history in our day as we give ourselves to the planting of churches and the discipling of all.

Action Steps

1. *Something to Discuss*

   a. How did the Early Church reach out in church planting?

   b. Discuss the parent-child characteristics that may be present in parenting a new church (advantages or problems). What difference in attitude can be noted in local church parenting as compared to a district-initiated project? Why?

   c. Which models of church planting appeal to you the most for your church and community, and why?

   d. When should your local church get involved in planting a new congregation?

   e. Discuss the apostle role as differentiated from other roles in churchmanship.

117

2. Something to Do

a. Find out how your district has been involved in home mission church planting and what future plans are in the making. How can you help?

b. Develop a plan as to how your church could develop a satellite structure for both expansion and extension growth. Decide what kind of outreach groups would work best in your church and community as satellite groups with a potential for church planting.

c. Do a socioeconomic study to determine the separate distinct groups of people in your community. Could a church be planted in each homogeneous unit?

3. Something to Read

Hurn, Raymond W. *Mission Possible.* Home Missions in the Church of the Nazarene as seen through "church-growth eyes."

Jones, Ezra Earl. *Strategies for New Churches.* The whole book.

McGavran, Donald A. *Understanding Church Growth,* pp. 285-92, church planting in cities in cross-cultural perspective.

McGavran, Donald A., and Arn, Win. *Ten Steps for Effective Church Growth.* Fascinating new insights into how the church at the local and national level can experience the growth it is capable of achieving.